Texas Tradition

By the Same Author:

Reverend Devil
Cavalier in the Wilderness

With Line Drawings by Nick Eggenhofer

ROSS PHARES

Texas Tradition

HENRY HOLT AND COMPANY · NEW YORK

Dedicated to

THE PIONEERS

*Who set the pattern for the
Texas tradition of courage,
ingenuity and free enterprise*

★

Preface

This is an account of the settlement and development of a new and untamed land, beset with wild beasts, savage Indians, and hostile foreigners; by a hardy, adventurous, down-to-earth people. These settlers were, in the main, already hardened, self-reliant frontiersmen from the American hinterlands.

In such an unsophisticated society, the people lived close to the real things of life, and they, in turn, were *real*. Thus their doings were the essence of human interest. They played, and laughed, and worked with gusto as individualists supreme. They fought and died recklessly and heroically, apparently without murmuring, as if the excitement of the gamble was worth the highest stake. They were, at times, rough, even brutal; but no crybabies were among them. There was a saying in Texas that the cowards never started and all the weak died on the road.

The Texans repelled the armies of Mexico and established a republic when the region was practically without a government, transportation, postal or monetary systems.

★

They fought for years to clear the land of savages, with virtually no help from government. Men drove cattle across the plains and mountains without the government guaranteeing them any protection. To have guaranteed the old adventurous cattleman a set price for his beef at the end of the trail probably would have insulted him. Men and women, who could not have understood the meaning of a government agency, settled farms and built homes with their bare hands. Here men and women had sufficient fortitude to work out their own destinies; they asked no quarter and gave none.

Their ingenuity produced some crude and humorous innovations; but they set a record for personal integrity, individual enterprise, and an exuberant freedom of spirit that people in our present mechanical, regimented, government-ridden, socialized age of assembly-line, mass-production, chain systems yearn for helplessly.

This account makes no claim to completeness, either in the selection of topics or treatment. No book could be big enough to hold the complete story of the Texas frontier.

Notes are used not merely for source references but also for bibliographical purposes for direction of readers who might desire to pursue the various topics further.

Much of the material has appeared in the author's syndicated column, *Texan Parade*. An account of Ad. Lawrence's ride appeared in *The Quarter Horse Journal*, the story of Sham Hays in *Swing* magazine, and numerous topics have appeared in the Dallas *Morning News*. This material is used by permission.

★

Contents

Texas Tradition

★

CHAPTER ONE

Customs

STRANGE WAYS

Travelers in frontier Texas reported many "strange" customs. Wayfarers often shared sleeping quarters with a dozen or more strangers. If a traveler retired late, he might see his bedfellow for the first time when he turned the covers back, or perhaps when he waked up the next morning and saw him in the light of day.

During a journey through Texas in 1856, Frederick L. Olmstead lamented on the lack of privacy for sleeping: "I hardly know whether to chronicle it as a border barbarism, or a Creolism, that we were several times, in this neighborhood, shown to a bed standing next to that occupied by the host and his wife, sometimes with the screen of a shawl, sometimes without." [1]

Olmstead told of his amusement at seeing a bed companion "gravely spit in the candle before jumping into bed." When questioned about this odd procedure, he explained that he always did so. It gave him time to see what he was about before it went out. [2]

★

Expectorating, Olmstead observed, was not only a perfected and practical art but, among the male population, was regarded about as necessary a function as breathing—and thus was generally prepared for. He attended one gathering at a courthouse, the floor of which had been strewn with sawdust to a depth of six inches—thus converting it into "one vast spittoon."

The occasion was a "March"—a joint celebration of Masons, Odd Fellows, and Sons of Temperance. After donning "various insignia of sashes and aprons" and forming behind a house, the procession marched out upon the square, where a Negro with a violin struck up a jig. After perambulating the square, the brethren marched into the courthouse; there, thanks to a thoughtful arrangements committee, cud-chewing continued uninterrupted and without extraordinary hazard to public property.[3]

Before the days of matches, pioneers were sometimes hard pressed to start a fire. One custom was to take a small rag, rub powder into it, ram it into a gun barrel, and then fire it out. The flash would ignite the powdered rag.

Many pioneers slept on bedsteads made in a corner of the cabin by placing one end of two poles in large auger holes in the log wall and the other ends placed on an upright log. "Springs" were made from laced rawhide. Dressed skins of buffalo, bear, or deer with the hair left on served as mattresses. Crystal in the homes was a rarity; but the country afforded an excellent variety of gourds that served practical purposes.

In 1834 A. A. Parker toured Texas gathering material for a book to serve as a guide for immigrants.[4] He entered the province by way of the San Antonio Trace. Before reaching San Augustine, he saw two racecourses and the only apple orchard he observed in Texas. At Nacogdoches, he found land to be "dog cheap." A Spaniard there had taken a liking to an American's dog, and when asked $100 for it he gave the American four leagues of land for the dog.

Parker noted that "corn is ground in a steel mill, like a coffee mill . . . having a crank on each side. This is commonly nailed to a tree before the door." It amused him to find that corn often was left standing in the field and gathered only as needed. To prepare the grain for food, it had to be gathered, ground, kneaded, and baked. He found one gristmill turned by horses.

He lamented that the people let the calves run with the cows, and therefore seldom had milk. He did not find butter at half the homes he visited, and only once obtained cheese in the province.

Coffee he found used in large quantities, but he found "hardly a cup of tea in the whole country."

For transportation, "baggage wagons are quite numerous, but I found only one pleasure carriage in the whole province, and that was a gig-wagon."

The most prominent fault of the inhabitants, he thought, was being "too fond of pastime and hunting." It appeared to him that the great concern of the people was "how they shall employ themselves to kill time." In the towns, "you generally find a billard room; and near it, a racecourse."

He saw no copper coins in circulation; and he knew of no bank in the province. He reported one happy financial aspect: "The inhabitants of the country pay no taxes at all."

★

Noah Smithwick furnished one of the first accounts of farming in Texas: "The soil, where there were vast cane-brakes all along the rivers, was rich and loose from the successive crops of cane that had decayed on it. In the fall when the cane died down, it was burned off clean. The ground was then ready for planting, which was done in a very primitive manner, a sharpened stick being all the implement necessary. With this they made holes in the moist loam and dropped in grains of corn. When the young cane began to grow, they went over it with a stick, simply knocking it down; the crop was then laid by." [5]

In the open country, many farmers planted their corn "Missouri style," by making a dent in the ground with the blow of an axe, dropping in the seed, and closing the hole by pressing down the earth with the foot.

J. C. Mann told of the difficulty of breaking land on the prairie: "So hard was the breaking of this land on man and teams, that the owner offered to give anybody an acre for every acre he would break. So any man who would, could get himself a prairie plow and about twelve yoke of oxen to pull it, and, with these and a good deal of hard work and scattered bits of profanity, he could own a good farm." [6]

One of the great problems of the pioneer farmers was keeping adequate dray animals. The Indians made it almost impossible in some sections to keep horses or mules. Many settlers abandoned them and adopted oxen instead.

One pioneer described plowmaking. He "would cut a short piece of some twisted oak tree, which would almost have the shape, split it open, then hew it down to fit the point of iron and attach the handles with wooden pins."

W. F. Cude told of pioneer farming implements: "Horse collars were made from shuck, plow lines from rawhide. Wagon wheels were sawed from sweet-gum logs."

Farming on the frontier was no get-rich-quick proposition. During one short crop year, a farm boy related: "We had corn for dinner and pa ate six acres of it."

TOBACCO

In the early days, it was a debatable matter among some groups, as to whether tobacco was a luxury or a necessity. The nicotine enthusiasts contended that it calmed a man's nerves and he got more work done while smoking or chewing—to say nothing of its worth for inducing contentment for meditative hours away from work. Many of the womenfolk insisted that a big washday without a few dips of snuff was beyond feminine endurance. So it was, on the frontier, that tobacco served as a stimulant, a sedative, a medicament, an insecticide, etc.

Smithwick observed that "Trading vessels came in sometimes, but few people had money to buy anything more than coffee and tobacco, which were considered indispensable." [7]

During Spanish days, the governments took advantage of the general addiction to tobacco by making it virtually a government monopoly by means of high taxes and other controls. This led to no end of smuggling and corruption of government officials, to say nothing of the added incentive for smoking and chewing. Many American settlers engaged in running tobacco past the officials to the tobacco-

★

craving Mexicans who bought it even when they could not buy food. Fortunes were made in the illegal trade.

There were few diversions from the hardships of the wilderness—a reason given for many of the inhabitants acquiring the tobacco habit at an early age. One writer related that he was amazed to see a little boy chewing tobacco and spitting juice like a veteran; but what really astonished him was that "the little fellow was so young he was still wearing dresses."

There is another story about children's use of the weed: A lady walking along the street one evening saw a boy leaning rakishly against a post smoking a cigarette. The child was so small that the woman's motherly instinct led her to approach him. She asked: "Young man, does your father know that you smoke?" The youngster took a couple more draws in silence, and then looked up at the lady out of the corners of his eyes and countered: "Madam, does your husband know that you speak to strange men on the street?"

Tobacco served as an insecticide in home, garden, and barn. Many women placed home-grown tobacco leaves in chicken nests to rid them of mites. Powdered tobacco was sprinkled on vegetables to kill garden pests. Tobacco "tea" was used to kill lice.

Tobacco was used extensively as a medicine—for toothache, jaundice, and dyspepsia. Tobacco poultices were applied to wounds to stop bleeding. Smoke was blown into ears to relieve earache. It was said that tobacco was good for corpulent persons in that it would make them "spit their fat away." Some parents testified that unhealthy children began to grow when they started using tobacco. The theory was that the poison of the tobacco counteracted poisons existing in their systems. One writer told of a man bitten by a rattlesnake who "had a chunk of tobacco in his pocket, which he chewed up, hastily binding it on the wound with his handkerchief, and went on his way, not losing a day's work." [8]

In the days before matches, it was often an uncomfortable task for a slow smoker to keep a pipe going. Smithwick told of going to investigate a cloud of smoke on the prairie one day, and upon reaching the scene found a man "lying half conscious in the midst of the cloud of smoke, his face blackened and burned, his clothing on fire, and his right arm almost torn from his body." The fragments of a powderhorn and a pipe lay nearby. When the fire had been put out, the victim, upon being questioned, explained the cause of the explosion. He said he "had lighted his pipe for a smoke, but the tobacco didn't burn well, so he turned up his powderhorn to add a few grains of powder for kindling." [9]

The extensive use of tobacco by cowboys is illustrated in an order made by the manager of the XIT Ranch. He "ordered a carload of cigarette papers as a winter's supply for his line riders." [10]

Cattleman Charles Goodnight spoke of the value of tobacco for men forced to go long periods without food: "I noticed that tobacco-chewers seemed to feel the hunger less than those who did not use it. It appears that tobacco had a tendency to stay the appetite."

Trail bosses took every precaution against running out of tobacco on the long cattle drives where armed men might become irritable when out of tobacco.

Substitutes were resorted to. One old-timer spoke of an emergency: "At the ranch, there was a big mesquite stump

★

in front of the mess-house that the cook used to knock the grounds out of the pot, and they had accumulated around it for weeks. The boys scraped up all these and smoked them." [11]

In *The Cowboy*, Rollins stated that often tobacco odor aided scouts in trailing men. "An excessive user of tobacco might have all his belongings so permeated with the weed's smell that his handkerchief or piece of cloth lying in the way would speak more definitely to the nose of the scout than to the latter's eyes." [12]

There has always been a lot of preaching against tobacco without any noticeable results. In order to help the women in a small Texas town save a new church carpet from tobacco juice, Evangelist Sam Jones, said at the beginning of his sermon: ". . . I did not come here to deliver an anti-tobacco lecture, and if I had I wouldn't expect to get anywhere with a lot of old billy goats like you. I am not asking you to quit chewing tobacco. . . . If you have a fresh chew in your mouth when you get here and don't want to lose the tobacco, if that is the idea, just take it out of your mouth and put it on a chip and lay it outside by the doorstep and you can get it when you get out of church. It will be there. There isn't a dog in the world that would touch it; there isn't a hog in the universe that would come within ten feet of it if he knew what it was. But I'll tell you, Bud, you'd better mark your chip; some man might get it." [13]

DANCING

Dancing was the chief social event of the frontier—the main boy-meets-girl arrangement. Everybody was invited. There was nothing exclusive on the frontier—no social register nor engraved invitations existed. The boss and the hired man were social equals at a party. It was open house from the first tune-up to rooster-crowing time.

Music was usually furnished by a fiddler, "seconded" by a guitar player. For added rhythm, a third party might "beat the strings" of the fiddle, as it was played, with a light stick or heavy broom straw. A clevis was sometimes beat with its pin as a percussion instrument.

One observer wrote of a dance: "When young folks danced those days, they danced; they didn't glide around; they 'shuffled' and 'double shuffled,' 'wired' and 'cut the pigeon's wing,' making the splinters fly. There were some of the boys, however, who were not provided with shoes, and moccasins were not adapted to this kind of floor (puncheons), and moreover they couldn't make noise enough. Their more fortunate brethren were not at all selfish or disposed to put on airs; so, when they had danced a turn, they generously exchanged footgear with the moccasined contingent and gave them the ring."

If the cowboy had "Sunday" clothes he wore them. If not, he went along in his range outfit; but he was always considerate. He held the lady's right hand in his left and put his right arm about her, but he always held a large handkerchief in his right hand to keep from soiling her dress.

There were always more men than women at the dances. At the larger dances, men were sometimes given numbers to designate their turn on the floor. Sometimes they had to wait until the small hours for their call. When the scarcity of women was critical, a white scarf might be tied on a man's arm, marking him as a "lady fair" to make up for

★

the deficiency. This was called "heifer branding." Normally it furnished more excitement for spectators than for participants.

Sobriety was required. There was no taking liberties with ladies to be excused by "I'd had too much to drink." Cowboys drank lots of "redeye," but they never got that drunk and privilege-taking—not with friends and relatives of the lady roaming about with loaded six-shooters.

The hostess usually set a room apart at dances for babies. One or more mothers took turns as baby sitters while the others danced. Sometimes cowboys helped with this chore while waiting for their numbers to be called. If no room for this purpose was provided, the infants might be bedded down in a wagon bed.

LOVE-MAKING

Possibly no enterprise portrayed the temper and color of the rugged, isolated frontier more realistically than the efforts of love-making. Volumes have been written to illustrate the shyness of the cowboy as a lover. He has been pictured as a Tarzan among the beasts, but a Mr. Milquetoast in the parlor. Actually, his courting manners were an odd mixture of bravado and timidity. Often affairs of the heart were started with the strictest formality. A young man wishing to make a date to take a girl to a dance might make his desire known by this rather fixed form—on the very best stationery, of course:

"Compliments of Mr. John Doe requesting the pleasure of escorting Miss Jane Smith to the dance at Centerville Saturday night."

The reply required the same formality:

10

"Compliments returned and the company of Mr. John Doe accepted by Miss Jane Smith for the dance at Centerville."

Whatever may have been the shortcomings of the backwoods swain, he was generally considerate in important matters. Big Foot Wallace was engaged to be married. In the meantime, he contracted typhoid fever that caused his hair to fall out. He said: "I'm not going to hold any woman to an agreement to marry me, with a head like a hard-boiled egg." So Wallace stayed in the wilderness rubbing his scalp with bear's grease trying to coax his hair back. As soon as he had sprouted a fuzz sufficient to promise a respectable covering, he set out to the home of his prospective bride; but while Big Foot had been massaging his pate with bear's grease, his fiancée had married someone else.

The frontiersmen, as a rule, were not without sentiment; but most of the mature ones had learned to live without women. Therefore, they were not, generally speaking, the type to "jump at the first chance," or easy to catch on the rebound. The story is told that Wallace, after living in captivity of the Lipans, was tied to the stake one day and brush piled around him preparatory to his being burned. At that moment, so the improbable account states, an Indian woman came rushing to him, a blanket thrown over her head, saying that she claimed him as her husband, as an exchange, according to tribal law, for her former husband who had been killed.

Then, to appeal to Wallace, she dropped the blanket from about her face. Wallace took one short look and said: "Come on and light your fire!"

★

Courting often necessitated considerable traveling. To transport a girl to a dance, in the West a man might ride fifteen miles to hire a buggy, travel the same distance to get the girl, another fifteen or twenty miles to the dance, then back to the girl's home, back to deliver the buggy, and then finally to his home, a total of perhaps one hundred miles.

In some matters, the frontier girls got fewer surprises from their husbands after marriage. Usually, she at least knew how he looked in his work clothes—and how dirty they would be on washday. There is an account of two cowboys on a drive who stopped at a ranch house and were asked by the girls if they were going to the dance. They replied: "Yes, where is it?"

The cowboys turned their cattle into the pasture, rounded up the girls' horses and went to the dance wearing the clothes they had been working in for six weeks. One of the boys found an old Prince Albert coat in the bunkhouse, and was thoughtful enough to wear this over his dirty shirt.[14]

Western fiction has given the idea that the "silent," "stammering" cowboys didn't get around much, that they could not think of anything clever to say in the presence of a lady. They did all right. Take the case of this prince charming in chaps from the sage-brush country: A lady left her overshoes at his ranch while attending a dance. Next day, he rode over to the girl's ranch, entered the parlor, and called for her. At her approach he pulled a shoe, wrapped in brown paper, from his pocket. "Here's something you forgot," he beamed.

"Oh, my overshoe!" she exclaimed. "But I had two."

"I know," the cowboy said. "I'll bring the other one tomorrow. And Miss ——, I just wish you was a centipede." [15]

The bashful cowboy could, on occasion, become as bold as any modern "wolf," once some gal got his dander up. Olcutt Sanders, in *The Sky Is My Tipi*, tells of a dance at Quanah where a cowboy became riled because the apple of his eye was dancing continually with a hand from another ranch. And no insisting for a dance on his part was effective. So, finally, during an intermission, he took the reluctant lady outside to a corner of the house where the rain had filled a tub, now frozen over. He set her down upon the ice and with hands grown strong at wrangling calves chugged her up and down until the ice broke. Then he told her kindly but firmly that it was for her own good and to cool her off. [16]

The doings of lovers have always stimulated a lot of talk from the spectators, often causing trouble. One frontier couple was seen hugging and kissing. The girl, a member of the church, was brought before that body to be disciplined for her bold actions with the young sinner. After a long and heated discussion, the examining committee turned to the old grandmother of the church, whose character was beyond reproach, saying that they would abide by her decision.

She was reluctant, but finally she rose and gave her opinion on the love-making matter. She said that she believed that "if there was more of it done and less said about it, the world would be better off." [17]

13

MARRIAGE

During pioneer days, getting married was not the simple process of finding a girl who would say "Yes." After the boy found the girl, he might realize it was harder to get a license, and still more difficult to locate someone to tie the nuptial knot. Texas was a Spanish land when the first Americans came; and there were many proverbial "old Spanish customs" to be complied with—one of them being that couples must be united in wedlock by a Catholic priest . . . or they weren't united.

Once Americans started flocking into Texas, there were not enough priests to take care of the marriage business. If love and marriage are what makes the world go around —as some philosopher has observed—certainly Texans were never ones to stop it, or even to slow it down. A good portion of the immigrants came to Texas in a hurry; and, from the Spanish point of view, they got married in a hurry.

Besides the inconveniences caused by the scarcity of priests, long distances had to be traveled to make marriage arrangements, and there was a fee of $25 charged for the ceremony in this money-scarce country. Thus, it is understandable that settlers made the best arrangement possible under the circumstances. Smithwick described the condition: "The father made a tour of the colonies occasionally when in need of funds. . . ." But usually, "when a couple concluded to join their fortunes, they forthwith repaired to the alcalde's office and had him draw up a bond to avail themselves of the priest's services whenever he came around; both parties signed the bond and went on their way as man and wife." [18]

This simple arrangement also made divorce a simple proceeding—avoiding the time and expense of Spanish legal red tape. If the couple changed their minds before the priest came around, they went to the alcalde, demanded the bond, tore it to pieces, and went their free ways again.

Sometimes, the couples had sizable families by the time the priest finally came around. It was nothing unusual in those days for parents to be married by a priest in the presence of a family of children. Sometimes, there were mass weddings, in which many couples assembled, for the convenience of the priest, to be married in one big wedding ceremony.

Orthodox settlers who were sticklers for form, often were confused and uncomfortable with these arrangements.

★

T. U. Taylor told of such a couple: "John Litton and Sarah Standifer were married under the Mexican flag, but Texas changed its political complexion so often that Sarah wanted to run no risk in regard to the legality of her marriage with John Litton and each new flag brought a new ceremony. . . Five times they were married—under five of the six flags that have waved over Texas." [19]

The inconvenience caused by Spanish laws led to the adoption of some novel ceremonies. "Jumping the broomstick" was common. For this ritual, the couple stood together, witnesses held the stick a foot or so above the floor or ground, and the pair hopped over together. Usually, this jump was made to the accompaniment of a song that served for the reading of the wedding vows. This was an old custom long practiced among the slaves in the South.

After the days of the Republic, there still were not nearly officials enough to take care of the marriage business. Judge Roy Bean served a vast territory west of the Pecos. His ceremonies were definitely without the peal of bells, the perfume of orange blossoms, or the throwing of rice. Long veils and long ceremonies were not common on the frontier. These words he considered adequate for joining man and woman in holy wedlock: "I, Roy Bean, Law West of the Pecos, by the authority vested in me by the Constitution and the laws of the State of Texas, do hereby pronounce you man and wife. And may God have mercy on your souls!"

Bean was a man of imagination and could vary a ceremony to suit an emergency. On one occasion, when members of two prominent local families were to be married, the ceremony was delayed because the train bringing the license from the county seat, Del Rio, was late. The wedding feast had long been in readiness, and Bean was hungry. So he united the two with a ceremony concluding: "By virtue of the authority vested in me by the State of Texas and the marriage license coming in on No. 10, I now pronounce you man and wife."

Securing a license was often a burden and an inconvenience. Dr. R. B. Buckner told of performing a ceremony for a young Negro man and woman, which seemingly inspired another couple in the audience to take the same step without delay. The would-be groom came to Dr. Buckner and asked him if it would be all right for him to borrow the license of the newly wedded couple and bring his sweetheart and get married without further bother.

The story is told of another couple that came to a minister late one Saturday night without a license. The minister told them that he could not marry them then—telling them to come back Monday. The young fellow asked: "Couldn't you just say a few words to tide us over the week end?"

Stanley Vestal tells of a cowboy who fell in love with a nester's daughter who was willing to marry him, but insisted upon a proper wedding. No preacher was within a day's ride. So the boys got together, organized, and elected one of their number justice of the peace. "In the cowcamp, there was no book but the brand book, but the J. P. was undaunted. Using the brand book as a Bible, he improvised a ceremony to the satisfaction of all concerned. The cowboy 'put his brand' on his bride, and the two were 'hitched to run in double harness.'" [20]

★

Settlers, particularly cowboys, were as practical in their speech as they were in their ceremonies. It was said of one newly wed cowboy: "Buck Smith has roped a heifer for life. He corralled her back East." One cowboy who married a girl from an adjoining ranch said: "All I had to do was drag her across a barbed wire fence."

GUN ETIQUETTE

Most cowboys were careless about their dining-room and parlor manners; but they were tediously careful about their gun etiquette. No one except a fool, or the completely uninformed, risked offending a man who packed a loaded six-shooter. Under the circumstances, one observed the rules of frontier niceties, went back East, or died young. For demanding respect, ancestry and money have never had the appeal of a convenient side arm.

When drinking, courtesy required that the armed man fill his glass, and, in carrying it to his lips, use his right hand—that is, his gun hand.

Rollins wrote: "As an incident to greetings between strangers, it was good form for each to bow to the extent of temporarily removing his hat, or at least to raise his right hand to his hat's brim. This took the theoretically dangerous hand away from the gun's position at the belt." [21]

Though a man might enter a dwelling house without removing his hat except during the moments of a bow or two, it was considered bad taste to enter the house wearing pistols. The considerate cowpuncher unfastened his belt and, with the attached holsters, usually hung it over the horn of his saddle.

Among mounted armed men, the proper procedure for dismounting was so to maneuver the horse that the rider came to the ground on the "open" side, not with the horse between him and another party.

If a man turned out to one side when meeting another rider, without giving some greeting, he made himself liable to suspicion. If an officer of the law met such a man, this was usually considered grounds for taking a shot at him. Men with six-shooters at their finger tips were not to be ignored under any circumstance.

If an informed rider in the open country saw a man waving his hat in a circle in the distance, he knew this meant to detour unless he was prepared to shoot it out. The signaler might have a neighbor's calf down under a running iron. The signal offered the approacher the courtesy of a choice—shoot or travel.

Most frontier peace officers were good shots. When one could wing a "tough customer," it was considered unprofessional and unethical to shoot him fatally. "Bluffing" was another word for suicide. Any gunman who drew, indicated that he meant business and had to be ready to shoot—quick. In a country where every man went armed, men were considerate of others' feelings. They had to be.

UNPLEASANTRIES

On the frontier, it was the custom to make a joke of anything unpleasant, including death. In the border country, killings were regarded as a natural course of events, and settlers learned to take them philosophically and laugh at what could not be avoided or regulated.

When asked why he had immigrated to that section,

★

an old-timer in Big Springs replied: "Nearly all of us came to this country because we had killed a carpetbagger or to keep from killing one." [22]

There had to be a way of ridding society of its enemies, even before the establishment of courts of law. The following statement of a pioneer minister might sound cold-blooded or ludicrous today; but the humor doubtless was unintended then. When asked: "What do you folks in this part of the country think of the killing of So-and-So?" the minister replied: "I have never known of a killing that gave such general satisfaction."

Sudden death at the hands of the Texas Rangers was regarded as routine business. The idea of anyone so stupid as to make a play for his gun in the presence of a Ranger was usually regarded as more humorous than sad.

A quotation from Rollins illustrates: "The ranger came up and said quietly: 'You're wanted. You'd better come along peaceful-like.' The outlaw began to throw talk. . . The ranger said . . . 'Come along with me.' The outlaw, still jawing, started to reach . . . and that outlaw stopped plumb short talking to the ranger and began a conversation with Saint Peter." [23]

Ben Thompson seemed to have had his greatest fun when out for a kill. He enjoyed making "witty" remarks about his handiwork. Fred E. Sutton quotes Thompson's explanation of firing three shots into a man when the first one killed him: "The first shot was to make him fall; the second was a precaution in case the first did not finish him —it was to catch him as he fell; the third was to scare the gang in the saloon." [24]

The death of a card cheat was often considered more

humorous than tragic. A coroner reported a gambler's demise thus: "Cause of death: Five Aces."

On the reckless, dangerous frontier, men took long chances. Here, they considered laughter a better tonic than crying. Because, what could not be remedied had to be endured.

★

CHAPTER TWO

Animals

WILD-ANIMAL HAZARDS

The pioneers lived close to nature, which meant that they lived in close harmony or disharmony with animals—wild and domesticated. One of the worst menaces along the waterways, where most of the first pioneers settled, were alligators. These reptiles not only caught domesticated animals, such as hogs and dogs, they attacked people as well. Smithwick related a story illustrating the habits of alligators: "When the alligator went foraging under cover of night, he evinced a decided preference for human flesh, particularly Negroes, and many blood-curdling stories are told of alligators stealing into sleeping camps and seizing an inmate." One night while a party of immigrants was camped at the mouth of the Brazos, on their way to Austin's colony, they were aroused by loud screams, and rushing out to the source of the disturbance "they found a huge alligator making for the river, dragging a 14-year-old Negro girl by the arm. He had crawled into the tent where a number of persons were sleeping, and whether from accident or choice, I cannot say, seized the darky and struck a beeline for the river, which he would have reached on

22

time with his prey but for his inveterate foes, the aforesaid dogs, who rushed upon him, and though finding no vulnerable point of attack, swarmed around, harassing and delaying his retreat till the men pulled themselves together and came to the rescue. Seeing the odds decidedly against him, his alligatorship relinquished his prize and sought his own safety in the river." [1]

Even children had to know what to do, quickly, in order to survive in the wild country. One day, the children of Charles Falenash were playing about a pond near their pioneer home on the river above San Felipe. One little boy waded out into the water. In a few minutes he let out a loud yell. His brother, John, looked out from the bank and was horrified to see that an alligator had hold of the child's leg. Knowing that the alligator would soon make for deep water, John drew his knife and dashed into the pond to the rescue, without taking time to try to call for help. He knew that the eyes were the only vulnerable points on the alligator. So he began stabbing at the reptile's eyes. It was a determined fight on both sides. Both the alligator's eyes were blinded before he released his hold. This done, however, John Falenash carried his little brother to the bank and to safety. [2]

Domesticated animals often had to fight for existence. N. L. Spence told of a fight between a hog and an alligator: "These wild hogs would tackle anything. One time I saw a mother hog (a sow) take her litter of pigs to the edge of the Neches River to drink. While they were drinking an alligator caught one of the pigs. Every hair on the sow's body stood up like an electric bristle. She jumped on that alligator in the shallow water and what a fight they

★

had. She finally dragged him to the land and made him give up the pig." [3]

Wild cattle knew much more about protecting themselves from beasts, such as wolves, than did domesticated animals. Gentle cattle were inclined to break for the safety of home when frightened, thus leaving unfortunate stragglers to the mercy of hungry attackers. Wild cattle, on the other hand, when attacked, would form a circle around their calves and thus present a line of horns for the wolves to face.

A pioneer woman in East Texas had completed the family wash on a creek three miles from home, tied the clothes in a bundle, placed them on her saddle horse with herself, and started home when a panther sprang out of the bushes and took after her. She put spurs to her horse and tried to outrun the panther, but he continued to gain on her. In desperation, she thought of a means to stay him off. She pulled a garment out of the bundle and threw it into the trail. The animal stopped and proceeded to tear it to pieces. This finished, he set out after her again. The woman dropped another garment, and again the panther stopped to tear it to pieces. This procedure was repeated again and again, each garment permitting the woman precious time to gain on her would-be attacker. She finally arrived home, with the family wardrobe much depleted, but without a single scratch. [4]

RATTLESNAKES

It was their great number, nearly everywhere, that made rattlers such a problem. Charles Goodnight said of the Pecos country: "Rattlesnakes were there by the thou-

24

sands and still are." One of his cowboys collected 72 sets of rattles in one season. A. A. Parker, in his report on Texas in 1834, stated that he saw one man who had killed 45 snakes in one day.[5] Oran Warder Nolan told of two ranchers in McMullen County who lost 35 calves during one season from rattlesnake bites. The previous year, the country had been plagued by rats coming up from the coast. It was surmised that the snakes were following the rats.[6]

Wallace Franks, a foreman on the Stockton and Walton Ranch southwest of Corpus Christi, related that he killed 14 in the cotton fields in one day. One farmhand, after chopping cotton, threw down his hoe before the day was done and told the foreman: "I happen to know the number of snakes you have to the row in this field. I have killed four to the row. So I am leaving." [7]

Possibly no living thing inspired more superstition on the frontier than the rattler. One of the most common beliefs was that a rattlesnake will not crawl over a hair rope. Many traveling pioneers placed grass ropes around their pallets when sleeping on the ground and slept without fear of reptiles. Their deliverance was due to luck or some other factor. It has been proved that a rattlesnake will not travel even a few inches to avoid crawling over such a rope. Rattlers do not hesitate to crawl over prickly substances. They are, however, inclined to avoid human beings and their odor. The theory has been advanced that the snakes may have refused to cross the ropes because they carried the odor of people, due to handling. If this theory is true, clothes or bedding might have served as well, or even better.

It was generally believed that prairie dogs, small owls,

★

and rattlers live together in the same hole. Owls and rabbits do use the holes of prairie dogs, but after the dogs have abandoned them. Charles Goodnight reported: "When the rattler enters, his intention is to swallow the prairie dog, which he does; and my observation is that a dog will not enter his hole when there is a rattler in it, which he probably knows by scent." Goodnight stated that he had placed dead rattlers in holes, and later found them thoroughly covered with dirt. It was his belief that the dogs tried to cover the holes when they knew a snake was inside. For, as he said, "If you slowly pour dirt in on a rattler, he will make his appearance promptly." [8]

Old-timers claimed that a rattlesnake could grow another fang in the event he lost one. This seems to be the case, though actually it is not true. Behind each of the large front fangs is a succession of smaller reserve fangs that become functional, in order, as their predecessors are lost.

It was generally believed on the frontier that one could tell the age of a rattlesnake by the number of joints in the rattle. It is true that each time the serpent molts a new ring and button are added; but a well-fed snake may slough three or four times a year. Also, the rings sooner or later become worn out and drop off.

Many stories prevail about the pilot snakes piloting the rattler. About the only known connections is that they haunt the same places and eat similar food. A few other erroneous sayings: The pilot snake is a "neuter" rattlesnake that devotes its time as a scout for the rattler. It is a companion snake for the rattler, traveling with it for company. It is a hybrid resulting from a cross between the rattlesnake and bull snake. [9]

A wide difference of opinion has been expressed about the habits of this snake. Goodnight believed that the rattlesnake did not move at night. If a cowboy found a rattler while riding guard at night, he could wait until morning to go and kill him.[10]

Most people, however, will not trust the rattler to cease his travels after dark. Olmstead stated that the rattler disliked to go through wet grass; that when the grass was wet the snake hung around the bushes or the edges of the roads. For this reason, the Texas Rangers chose high grass to spread their blankets on at night.[11]

Among naturalists, there is a difference of opinion as to whether snakes are susceptible to their own venom when it is injected into their blood. There are accounts, from reputable sources, of rattlers biting themselves and then dying. Some authorities contend that injury to the spinal nerve or some vital organ may have caused death rather than the poison. Most snake experts say that it is not probable that any snake ever intentionally commits suicide.[12]

One of the most effective natural enemies of the rattler was the wild turkey. August Santleben described a fight between the two. He was traveling the road near Uvalde when he saw a large flock of wild gobblers in an open glade, congregated in a circle fighting a rattler. "One after the other would spring into the air in rapid succession and come down on the reptile, which they struck a hard blow with one wing that might have been heard quite a distance. Apparently, all the gobblers took part . . . and they appeared to be greatly excited; but the hens fed quietly in the vicinity and seemed to be indifferent to what was going on." Santleben's presence frightened the gobblers away. When he approached the snake, it was coiled and almost dead. He stated that the turkeys, after killing the snakes, feasted upon them.

This writer related that deer were prejudiced against rattlesnakes and invariably attacked them in favorable localities. It seemed that the rattler feared the deer more than any other animal as "it makes no effort to strike but suffers a collapse under an instinctive fear that prompts it to submit to its fate with its head hid beneath the coils of its body, which are closely drawn together.

"The deer springs from a safe distance into the air with its four feet brought together and it comes down on the snake with his sharp pointed hoofs, which cut like a knife. The movements are rapid and often repeated until the rattler is mangled into a shapeless mass." [13]

Opinions have always varied as to the deadliness of the rattler. Some people think that it is fear and resulting shock more than the venom that kills. Nolan told of a conversation with Dr. M. M. Poole who said that he had "treated scores and scores of snake-bitten people" in every stage and condition, but "I have never seen anyone die from snake-bite. . . . The main service of a doctor is needed to ward off the shock. . . Nature removes the poison. . . The very act of breathing removes it. . . The blood system throws the poison into the stomach, and that's why some of them [victims] become nauisated." [14]

People can form antibodies that will resist venom of rattlesnakes. Mrs. Martha Odell, of San Antonio, who traveled with a side show, stated that she had been bitten by poisonous snakes about eleven hundred times over a period of 30 years. The first bite (accidentally) troubled her, the successive bites became less and less severe until she was gradually immune.[15]

Next to avoiding the rattler, the big problem is to find and administer a cure for its bite. Olmstead reported the main remedies on the frontier to be ammonia and whisky. A favorite remedy among the Mexican population was to make an incision with a Spanish dagger. Goodnight reported that the Texas Rangers "scarified the wounds with deep incisions and packed them full of salt." Some victims took hasty and drastic remedies. One cowboy bitten on the tip of a finger, drew his six-shooter and blew off the finger at the second joint.[16]

BEARS

The bear is a symbol of rugged, independent life, and therefore has been the subject of much frontier literature. He is also pictured as a frightful, deadly monster, whose chief instincts are to claw and eat human beings. In spite of the many campfire tales to the contrary, the bear rarely attacks a human being unless defending its young, or when attacked or cornered.

Probably the most popular myth about the bear is that it hugs its enemies to death. Bears have been trained for exhibition purposes to box and wrestle; but, according to most authorities, they show no natural tendency to hug or clench an antagonist.

James A. McKenna recorded some characteristics of the bear in his autobiography, *Black Range Tales*, as follows: "The bear's teeth are made for vegetable, rather than for fleshy, foods. . . . They are smart beasts but do not rank

★

as high in that respect as a dog or horse. . . . During the breeding season, they seem to carry a chip on their shoulders." [17]

McKenna told of the natural peacefulness of bears. He was sitting in the doorway of his cabin when he saw in the distance what he took to be two dogs rolling on the ground. After a while, he went to them and found the animals to be two bears about six months old. "They ran toward me, frisking and tumbling around my legs." He tried to drive them off, afraid that an angry, defending mother might attack him; but the cubs refused to go away. McKenna concluded that the mother had been killed. The cubs trailed him back to his cabin and became devoted pets. They learned to dance and wrestle with him. [18]

Bears attack stock for food, but unlike members of the cat family, they often depend upon cunning rather than stalking. Bears have been observed rolling in the grass and waving their tails to attract cattle and lure them through curiosity close enough to spring upon them.

Old Bruin has furnished much fun to members of the human race as the subject of jokes, many of which have made him appear more vicious than he actually is. He has also been the victim of jokes, which indicates that he can usually be handled satisfactorily, if the teaser is prepared.

J. Evetts Haley tells of cowboy Frank Mitchell lassoing a bear and bringing him into camp. There the cowboys decided to put the JA brand on him. A cowpuncher roped the bear's heels and stretched him out between two horses. The branding iron was heated. Then Mitchell put it to the bear's hip and turned him loose.

The resulting commotion indicates that bears may have

caused more people to hurt themselves than the bears have hurt. The bear broke through the door of the nearby kitchen where Mrs. Dever was washing dishes, her baby resting in a crib beside her. At the approach of the beast, she grabbed the child and pitched it out the window, fainted, and fell into the woodbox behind the stove. The bear jumped onto the table, ran up it and jumped out the window. Men were running in every direction. The baby was stepped on; and, as the animal ran down a trail, he stampeded the hired help in that direction. The bear apparently made no effort to harm anyone, but he was hardly in a friendly mood with his rump freshly seared by a hot branding iron.

Instinctively, Old Bruin is shy and timid, and prefers to go his own way unmolested; but he is a tough creature with whom no sensible, unprotected person will take liberties.

The frontiersmen were not inclined to study the bear scientifically. When possible, they let him have his way while they held their distance. Few people cared to investigate the probability of the tall tales Old Bruin inspired.

SKUNKS

In the parlance of the West, the skunk is the symbol of things bad. The pioneers found the skunk not only an annoyance and a nuisance, but frightfully dangerous, because the skunk was a potential bearer of hydrophobia. A bite by an affected animal in those days usually meant the most horrible death.

Unlike the bear and wildcat, he was not averse to inviting himself to sleep under a camper's blanket. Many

★

cowboys and miners have waked up on a crisp morning to find one of the striped-backed creatures cuddled up to his warm side like a house cat. These were occasions when the contemptible polecat received the gentle, considerate treatment due a house guest—for a brief time. Dogs were about the only reliable protection against these nocturnal visitors.

Billy Dixon, famed scout and buffalo hunter, possibly summed up the sentiment of the Plainsmen when he said: "I would have preferred being bitten by a rattlesnake." [19] The skunk was a particularly terrifying nuisance because he might appear perfectly healthy and yet be a carrier of the deadly disease.

The Indians claimed that the animal did not cause hydrophobia among their members. However, they reported cases of blindness caused by the spray of the "varment."

Getting rid of a skunk was usually a tedious problem. Killing him with a bullet was something like taking a chance against a quick-drawing, dead-aim gunman. You may get in the first shot and still lose.

McKenna tells of a method that worked for him one night when a skunk visited him in his cabin: "Someone had told me that a skunk would follow a lighted candle if it were held before its eyes. I told Drudgins to get in front of it and lead it to the door while I got ready to shoot it in the eye as soon as he had it into the right position. We were slow and quiet in every move we made, and we spoke in whispers in order not to excite the skunk. All our plans worked fine except . . . my bullet only creased the animal." [20]

Skunks thrive in a life of ease because, in the language of an old-timer, "nothing will mess with a polecat." Man, as well as carnivorous animals, give him a wide berth.

Stanley Vestal aptly described the skunk as a creature "which treads softly and carries a big stink." [21] Even so, many people claim that the animal makes an affectionate and devoted pet, which indicates there is no accounting for taste.

McKenna obviously did not dislike all skunks. He tells of petting a family of them: "One evening while I sat nodding before the fire, I was aroused by a catlike patter. Through the open door came Mrs. Skunk and her family. You may be sure I did not bother her. She picked up some scraps of meat and bread that cluttered the floor and out she went. For many nights after that, she made me a visit without in any way disturbing my comfort. She became very friendly, purring and rubbing my legs like a cat, while her kittens soon made themselves at home on my shoulder or in my lap. I called the mother 'Scraps,' and she learned to feed from my hand." [22]

Until the passing of a recent trade law, a fur coat with a Paris trade-mark labeled "monkey skin" may not have originated in the jungle. It could have been made of pole-cat hides from Texas. In the fur trade, until recently, skunk business was monkey business.

There was an old Western saying about a man in bad trouble: "He's got a skunk by the tail."

PRAIRIE DOGS

The prairie dog was the number one nuisance on the Plains in the early days. At one time, Texas had 90,000 square miles well covered with prairie-dog towns. [23] Over this vast area, the dogs ate grass and other valuable crops,

★

and made horseback traveling hazardous. Hundreds of cow ponies had to be shot as a result of stepping into a prairie-dog hole and breaking a leg; and many cowboys have been crippled for life as a result of a fall on such occasions.

The prairie dog is an alert, clever, self-reliant creature, and thus is hard to destroy. In the "town" a few sentinels sit on top of the higher mounds; and, at the approach of man or beast, they start barking warnings of danger.

There are two questionable uses of the prairie dog. First: Some people contend that he makes an enjoyable pet. Vestal went so far as to write an admiring poem about him. He said that to become a pet he should be caught as a pup. "But there is no nonsense about him. He likes his master because he likes company—and a good meal." [24]

Once when Charles Goodnight was swimming the Platte River with a herd of cattle, he found the stream full of prairie dogs headed for the south bank. He lifted one from the water and placed it behind his saddle on the horse's back. There the little animal rode until Goodnight reached the north bank. The dog was placed in the chuck wagon, and there he rode up the trail with the outfit. At night the cowboys took him from the wagon and turned him out to graze. Goodnight claimed that the animal made a most interesting pet and did much to break the monotony of the long drive. [25]

These examples are exceptions rather than the rule. Most people look on the prairie dog as a contemptible pest, whether on the loose or in captivity.

The other debatable use for the prairie dog is as food. The frontiersmen at times, when outside the buffalo range, ate these animals when they could find nothing else. It was often more difficult to bag a prairie dog than a buffalo. Hunters have claimed that with the dog's head shot off it would fall back in its hole and kick itself below the first bend. It took a lot of prairie dogs to make a meal for a group of hungry men. When fat, it was admitted, the animals made a good soup, but it was not very nourishing. Hunger came on again in two or three hours.

Texas Ranger Jeff Milton told of going into an eating house in Big Springs for a meal, and found the dish of the day to be "rabbit stew." When he questioned the waitress, she insisted that it was good rabbit stew. Milton blurted out that "any fool knows that rabbit bones ain't red." [26]

BUFFALOES

One of the saddest incidents in the history of the Old West was the destruction of the buffalo. Uncalculated millions of these animals ranged over approximately a third of the continent, where for unknown centuries they were the chief source of food, clothing and shelter for the natives. Yet, in approximately a decade—the 1870's—the white man wiped this source of life off the Plains.

Some say this was caused by civilization moving westward too rapidly; others say simply that it was greed of the white man; and those who try to justify everything in favor of the Caucasian say it was a noble measure to rid the country of the Indians by starving them out.

As a commercial proposition, the world has never known a waste of game equal to that of the buffalo slaughter. How many hunters came to the Plains hunting the buffalo for their hides can only be vaguely estimated. One hunter estimated that in 1876 there were 5,000 in Texas alone. Between 1871 and 1887, 5,860,000 hides were shipped from one railroad terminal—Dodge City.

Rarely was there any sportsmanship in the killings. It was a wild rush among bold and reckless men to get the one or two salable parts of the animal, strictly a business of mass destruction. It was big business, but not good business. The market was glutted; and the wholesale slaughter

of the herds netted only a small percentage of what they might have brought under thoughtful organization or control. Packers were late in realizing the superior quality of the meat. Then only a negligible percentage was saved.

The meat of an average buffalo selling at from two and one-half to three cents a pound would gross about $11. Many of the buffaloes brought only one dollar for their hides. Buffalo tongues sold as high as ten pesos in Mexico City; but few hunters thought about any part except the hide.

The stupidity of the buffalo made his extermination comparatively easy. Billy Dixon, one of the most noted of the hunters, observed that the buffalo "would pay scarcely any attention to white hunters, even though the big buffalo guns were booming from sunrise to sunset," though the appearance of an Indian would usually stampede a herd.

The characteristic of buffalo stupidity is revealed in an account by another famous buffalo hunter, Wyatt Earp: "A hunter would drag his Sharps to a rise of ground giving a good view of the herd, pick a bunch of animals, set his rest sticks and start shooting. He aimed to hit an animal on the edge of the bunch, the leader, if possible, just back of the foreleg and about one-third the way up the body. If the slug went true, the animal would drop in his tracks or stagger a few steps and fall. Strangely enough, the buffalo paid no attention to the report of the rifle and very little, if any, to one that fell.

"A first-class hunter would kill with almost every shot, and if he was good, he could drop game until some buffalo still on his feet chanced to sniff closely at one that had fallen. Then it was up to the hunter to drop the sniffer before he could spread the excitement over the smell of blood. If he could do this, the slaughter might continue, but eventually the blood scent became so strong that sev-

★

eral animals noticed it. They would bellow and paw, their frenzy would spread to the bunches near by, and suddenly the whole herd was off on a wild run." [27] As many as a hundred animals have been known to be killed in this fashion from one stand. *Earp* related that Billy Tilghman took 3,300 hides between September and April of one year.

A few buffaloes were killed for sport; but when the greenhorn appeared on the range, the professional hunters hustled him off if possible, upon giving him all the meat he could carry home, in order to keep him from stampeding and scattering the herds. Occasionally, tourists shot buffaloes from train windows just to see them fall. Buffalo Bill Cody killed 69 buffaloes on a horseback run just to show a few hundred excursionists what he could do.

After the hides were sold and the carcasses rotted, the final act of the tragedy was the collection and sale of bone. Thousands of tons of buffalo bone were collected and shipped for use as fertilizer and carbon.

The Indians have a legend about the sudden disappearance of the buffalo to the effect that the buffalo went down into the bowels of the earth where they still abound in a land called "Shipapu." They couldn't believe that mankind would or could destroy so completely and quickly the source of life on the Plains. It is a kind, ironic old legend that flatters the white man.

DOGS

Dogs have played a prominent part in the development of Texas—herding sheep on the Plains, trailing wild animals to provide meat for the pioneers, standing sentinel and fighting against savage Indians and other dangers.

Texas, from the beginning, has been a land of dogs—all kinds of dogs—and dog stories.

In 1719 a dog, in a strangely faithful and dramatic way, helped strengthen France's claim to Texas by saving the life of his master. A colony of Frenchmen landed on the coast of Texas. M. de Belisle, with his dog and four other officers, went into the woods to hunt. They became lost. When they finally returned to the sea, their ship had sailed. For several days they wandered along the coast hoping to sight their vessel, living during the time upon herbs and insects.

In desperation, the men begged Belisle to let them kill the dog for food. Belisle would not agree, though he was starving. The desperate men attempted to kill the dog anyway; but they were so weak that the dog—obviously sensing their designs—escaped and disappeared into the woods.

As the days passed, Belisle saw his four companions die of starvation, one by one. He subsisted mainly by eating worms from rotten wood.

One day as he sat on a log, despondent, and so weak he felt that his final day had come, he looked up and saw his dog before him, wagging his tail, as if afraid to approach without some assurance of security. When the dog approached, Belisle spoke to him and saw that he was carrying an opossum in his mouth "about the size of a sucking pig." The dog laid the opossum down at his master's feet. Belisle feasted on the opossum.

Whether the dog had followed Belisle at a distance, fearing to come closer or because of fear or resentment of his master's companions, Belisle could not say; but he gave

★

his dog credit for saving his life and doing a great service to France. Belisle finally made his way overland to the French colony in northwest Louisiana, and lived to lead another expedition back to the Texas coast. In the final analysis, if Spain instead of France got Texas, it was no fault of M. de Belisle and his dog, which, under the strangest and most hazardous circumstances, was ingenious enough to take care of himself and his master.[28]

Faithfulness and application to duty among sheep dogs are frontier legends. In 1876 the notorious outlaw, Sostenes L'Archeveque, shot one of the Casner brothers and his Indian sheep herder to death in the Palo Duro Canyon for Casner's gold. The Casner shepherd dog was guarding sheep when the Indian herder was attacked. The dog left his herding duties and rushed to the assistance of the herder and fought the attacker until a bullet brought him down.

About a week later, a couple of cattlemen rode into Palo Duro and found the wrecked camp and the bodies. The outlaw's bullet had not killed the dog; it had only knocked one eye out and stunned him. Though nearly starved, and in great pain, the dog was faithfully holding the sheep in herd.

Though cattlemen, at this time, violently hated sheepmen and almost everything associated with them, one of the men adopted this proved animal. Among cattlemen, he apologized for the animal's background; but in this rugged land where heroes were a necessity and admired as such, he never apologized for the "blood" in his dog.[29]

A prospector in the Elk Mountains came upon a large bunch of sheep herded only by dogs. The sheep were fat

40

and healthy, but for days the prospector observed that no human being ever appeared with them. The prospector later learned that the Indians had killed the herders and stampeded the flock. The dogs had rounded up the sheep and had driven them over a hundred miles to their original stamping grounds.

Dogs in this region were trained for such emergencies. A few goats were kept with the herds. Before the eyes of a prospective sheep dog were open, he was given to some nanny that had lost her kid. The goat usually adopted two or more pups and suckled them until they were able to shift for themselves. When the dogs grew up, they were taught to catch a nanny and milk her if necessary. One dog would hold her while the other sucked her. As long as there was a nanny in the herd, the dogs would not starve. Thus the dogs managed their sheep and goats and lived comfortably enough, bound by instinct and training never to leave a job undone.[30]

In 1870, near Hog Mountain Springs, dogs trailed a band of marauding Indians into a thicket. The dogs were tied while their masters surrounded the thicket and went about the mopping-up campaign. The dogs had been on the chase a long time. Two of them refused to be left out of the final battle. They broke loose and pressed an attack until both of them were shot with arrows. One dog died in the thicket. The other came out with an arrow shot through the breast protruding behind the shoulder. The wounded dog lay down and deliberately pulled the arrow out of his body. He recovered to fight again.[31]

During Indian fighting days, many dogs displayed an uncanny sense of danger and caution. J. Wright Mooar

★

often had to travel through Comanche country when the Indians were on the warpath. His dog, Towser, half wolf, slept at his head when he traveled alone. At the slightest disturbance, Towser would awaken him. He stayed constantly alert, and always silent. Yet at camp, out of danger, he made so much noise he was considered a nuisance.[32]

The Indians had such high respect for dogs as fighters that, at least on one occasion, they scalped one as a prize of war. At the famous Battle of Adobe Walls, the Shadler brothers were caught asleep in the initial attack and killed. Their big Newfoundland dog obviously put up a vicious defense; for he was found the next morning beside his masters filled with arrows and scalped.

Billy Dixon lost his beloved dog, Fannie, at this battle. A few months later, he returned to the scene with some companions, and much to his surprise Fannie appeared. He thought she had been killed by the Indians or had wandered off and starved. After Fannie had been petted and fed, she left; but soon she came back, holding something in her mouth, and standing before the man wagging her tail. Dixon wrote of the incident in his autobiography. It is a touching scene showing the tender love of a tough old buffalo hunter for his dog: "Fannie had brought a fat, bright-eyed little puppy in her mouth. Dropping the little fellow gently on a pile of bedding, she frisked about with delight as each of us tried to hold the pup and fondle it. Fannie bounded away while we were 'fussing' among ourselves to see who would play with the pup. She came back with another pup in her mouth." She made other trips and finally placed four pups on the bedding. "The father of these pups was the big Newfoundland that belonged to the Shadler brothers." [33]

These hardy outdoor men were touched by this dog family carrying on in the wilds like the true pioneer stock that they were—the enterprising mother and four sturdy pups fathered by a fighter who had died a hero's death defending his masters.

You may still find a dog owner in Texas who claims that his canine is a descendant of this stock. It's something like saying his own ancestors came over on the *Mayflower* or was one of the original Three Hundred. He will possess no papers to prove it, but no true dog lover can blame him for wanting to believe it. In Texas, ancestry is important, even among dogs.

HOGS

Little has been written about the "lowly" swine. The razorback, unlike the longhorn, just isn't the proper type "critter" to sing a ballad to. The hogpen is the very antonym of the wide-open spaces of the cattle range; but hogs played an important part in frontier economy.

A razorback has been described as "the thinnest possible piece of pork connecting a snout and a tail." Many of the razorbacks, however, did not have tails, the lack of which was explained in this fashion: They were cut off by the settlers because the animal in his native element, mud, gathered such a heavy ball on his long tail that it pulled the skin backwards from his snout so tightly that he could not close his eyes. Therefore, the tails just had to be bobbed in order for them to get any sleep.

43

★

The hog is not native to America. The first razorbacks in the South probably descended from "thirteen sows" brought over by De Soto in 1539. During the explorer's wanderings, the hogs multiplied. Many were lost and some traded to the Indians. La Salle obviously brought over another strain; for, when the Spaniards reached the site of his fort in 1689, they found wild hogs running about the ruins.

The razorback was a counterpart of the longhorn, whose descendants also escaped from the early Spanish explorers. By the time the American settlers came to this country, hundreds of generations of these hogs had produced a hardy, self-sustaining breed, adopted to the land through a process of "survival of the fittest." They served as a vital source of food for many of the pioneers. One settler wrote: "We used to go hog hunting like people hunt deer today, and kill wagonloads of them, some of the finest you ever saw."

These animals were fast on foot and fast and vicious with tusks. They had to be. Bears and panthers preyed upon them constantly. Coyotes and wolves stole pigs when they could find them separated from the sow; but no coyote or wolf could out fight a healthy, grown razorback. Usually, sows with pigs ran in bunches for the sake of protection.

The pioneers found hog raising about the safest of stock ventures. Indians could not run off hogs as they ran off horses. Neighboring cow thieves did not bother them. In East Texas the porkers usually fattened in the woods on the mast in the fall. During the summer and lean seasons, they usually rooted enough out of the ground to sustain themselves.

A fat hog is immune from snake bite.

Some people have given the razorback credit for great intelligence. These admirers claim that in the early fall, before mast time, he will clench grape vines in his jaws and shake the fruit from the tall timber. You can get an argument quickly on the subject of the razorback's intelligence.

There came a time in Texas when hogs were so much more valuable than cattle that beeves were slaughtered for hog feed. Richard King, of the famous King ranch, after several unsuccessful attempts to preserve beef, brought in several thousand hogs to eat the meat of beeves killed for their hides. He then marketed the fattened hogs. When cattle had to be driven great distances calves were useless. Ike Pryor told of killing five hundred calves at one time for hog feed.

There were hog drives much in the fashion of cattle drives; but they were rare in Texas. Youngsters often left home against parents' wishes to join a cattle drive as a cowboy; but this writer has never heard of any lad running away from home to become a hog boy. It would possibly take pages to explain this difference—but any hog raiser will understand.

The razorback may have gotten into the joke book instead of the classics, but he sustained many Texans when just staying alive was a full-time job on the frontier.

★

CHAPTER THREE

Horses

MUSTANGS

The frontier, to a considerable extent, was won by men on horses. Transportation, communication, and defense depended upon them. A man without a horse in the early days was practically a nobody. Possibly at no time and place have man and beast lived in such close communion. In Texas, the horse may have been "man's best friend."

The Spanish explorers introduced horses into Texas, where they multiplied into herds of thousands by the time the Americans came. Men hunted these wild, beautiful, useful creatures with determination and recklessness, sometimes resulting in the death of both.

"Creasing" was one of the most common methods of capturing mustangs. The horse hunter shot a rifle ball through the top of the animal's neck, stunning him and knocking him to the ground. Then, he quickly threw a rope around the animal's neck before he could recover.[1]

Mustangers herded multitudes of these fleet creatures

amid much racing and excitement, into pens built to hold them. This was the hard, reckless, wasteful method; for many of the animals were killed in this process or injured for life in their attempts to escape.

Daredevil mustangers roped and subdued the animals by the direct process of overpowering them. A man of patience "walked" his wild horses down. One old-timer related that his system was "to keep right after them in a walk, keeping up the same gait day and night, never allowing them to approach a water hole or take time to graze, and in due time he could drive them into his pens." This was usually accomplished by riders, in relays, on horseback; but, in some instances, men on foot walked horses down in this fashion, a feat not as difficult as it may

★

appear. For the mustangs roamed a regular range, and when they reached the limits of this range, no matter how closely pursued, they soon circled back.

CONTEST FOR HORSES

The contest for possession of horses caused the major trouble on the frontier between the whites and Indians. The Indians staged most of their raids to secure mounts, whether from another tribe or from the Americans.

Almost the first ordinance passed by the conquerors of New Spain prohibited any Indian from riding a horse. The Spaniards told fantastic and fearful tales about the animal —that the monster devoured human flesh. In spite of potential dangers, however, the Indians desired these creatures. In time, they learned to steal them from the presidios and missions and ride them to freedom. To the Indians, the horse became a symbol of freedom and was often called the "God-dog."

For an Indian to steal a horse from a fellow tribesman was the most disgraceful of crimes—worse than stealing his wife; but to steal one from the enemy, especially the whites, was a feat to be proud of and to advertise. The Comanche wore three kinds of insignia on his shield: bear teeth, indicating that he was a great hunter; scalps, showing that he was a mighty warrior; and horse tails, indicating that he was an accomplished raider. The latter was the most cherished "medal" the Indian buck could display. The Indian's great desire for horses inspired all sorts of artifices and risks.

Dogs were the frontiersmen's greatest aid in protecting stock. The barking of dogs usually alerted the household; but some wily Indians employed a ruse that got the dogs

out of the way. One Indian would come up from the opposite direction of the place where the horses were located,
and by attracting the attention of the dogs would lure
them off for some distance, while others of the band
stealthily took off the horses.[2]

J. Taylor Allen told of a band of Indians that came to
a settlement one night to steal horses and found them en-
closed in a corral made of poles, whose tops were bound
with iron-like ropes of rawhide. One Indian climbed
quietly into the enclosure with the end of a rawhide lasso
in hand. He at one end, and a companion on the other,
sawed the lasso back and forth until they cut the ropes.
Then they uprooted several of the posts and let the horses
out.[3]

Even a solid adobe wall was not sufficient to hold stock
against determined Indians. McKenna told of Indians
with a rawhide lariat sawing a hole in an adobe wall of a
corral big enough to let out horses. In order to speed up
the sawing, one Indian poured a steady stream of water on
the wall at the place of sawing, while two others drew the
rope back and forth.[4]

Men sometimes had horses stolen from them while
holding them with a rope. They fell asleep and some
stealthy buck slipped up, cut the rope, took the animal and
left the guarding owner holding the rope—or a piece of it.[5]

A settler in Jack County found that the only way he
could secure his horses during the light of the moon was
to lock them to trees with trace chains in the yard.[6]

An Indian would readily sacrifice a poor horse for a
good one. Colonel Richard I. Dodge told how Indians
raided horses from a well-guarded camp one night by a
novel stampede tactic. Suddenly, a huge ball of fire

★

swished into camp, accompanied by terrific yells of Indians. Through and among the horses the fire ball went, startling the animals so that many of them broke their strong fetters and disappeared in the darkness. No Indians appeared in sight and the camp settled down again for the night.

Next morning the soldiers discovered the remains of the mysterious, flaming phenomena—the dead body of a miserable pony, the outside skin and flesh burned to cinders. The Indians had bound grass and other inflammable material at hand all over the animal, and then led him in the darkness as near as they dared go to the line of sentinels, turned his head in the right direction, and then set fire to him.[7]

A tale persisted on the frontier to the effect that the Indians trained wolves to gnaw the stake ropes of horses so the Indians could steal them.[8] Considering the passion the Indian possessed for good horses, he possibly tried everything he could think of. The Indian had such high regard for his mount that he tied a bag of his good medicine in its tail.[9]

To men on the frontier, white and red, success and preservation of life often depended upon the intelligence, stamina and speed of the horses they rode. Every true frontiersman knew this, and thus selected and maintained his horse with the greatest possible care.

HORSE SENSE

Many old-timers on the range insist that the horse is the most intelligent of animals. Some claimed that Indians and horses, because both were closer to nature, understood each other better than white men and horses understood each other. This is doubtful. Though horses respond to intimacy, they also respond to superior and technical training.

Certainly, the Indians adapted horses to their peculiar uses in remarkable ways. They used them as "watch dogs." White Wolf, of the Comanches, told how his horses were trained to stand as sentinels while their master butchered buffalo. Butchering was a hurried and intense business, upon which a man could not well concentrate while keeping a lookout for danger; but with a trained horse at hand, a quick glance at the animal's ears kept the skinner informed. The horse waved his ears alternately if another buffalo or coyote was close. If a man approached, he pitched both ears forward.[10]

Horses acted not only as sentinels against the approach of white men, horses of white men gave warnings by snorting and jumping at the scent of an Indian. For some reason, this reliability for warning was rather general, not just among horses that had been shot in battle, or otherwise injured by the opposite race.

Some admirers claim that horses, particularly those in the wilds, possess an unusual ability to reason when faced with emergencies or unusual situations. In swimming a river, the colt is maneuvered to the downstream side of its mother which serves as a breakwater. Colts have been seen to place the head over the back of a grown animal and float across a stream.

On the long Western cattle drives, the horses used for night guard learned their duties quickly. Cowboys have attested that a rider could fall asleep or doze in the saddle, but his horse would maintain the correct distance in his leisurely, sentinel rounds. If trouble arose, the mount gave adequate warning by his movement.[11] Most of these horses possessed a more accurate sense of time than their riders. When the time came to change the guard, many of them would clamp the bits in their mouths and head for the chuck wagon.

A trail driver named Chester Evans owned a horse that would "ride herd" over the *remuda*. If an outlaw horse broke away from the bunch, he would grab the unruly animal by the neck and bring him back to the drove.[12]

J. Frank Dobie, in *The Mustangs*, tells of a horse he rode named Buck which was a "catch dog." Buck would go for a halting cow with mouth open and grab her just forward of the tail bone if she did not move on. This horse was also used for trailing. By scent, he could find cattle attacked by screw worms.[13]

It is probable that the horse has a keener sense of smell than the dog. Many people have used them to trail animals, including deer. How reliable, temperamentally suited, or otherwise practical they might be for this type of activity possibly has never been thoroughly tested.

Some horses learn the ways and habits of their master faster than the master learns theirs. One pioneer had a horse that pulled him about in a buggy. A dependable animal, he stood without being hitched—any place, that is, except in front of a saloon. He had learned something of the delaying nature of business transacted in saloons. When left in such a locality, he waited until his master was inside the door, shook his head, and then went home to his stable and waited there to be unharnessed.[14]

Smartness often leads to figurative illustrations (usually exaggerated). Some ranchers have claimed that they owned horses so smart they could read brands. If they had a herd of cattle of mixed brands and wanted a certain brand cut out, all they had to do was let the horse know which brand was wanted cut out and the horse would sort them out. As to cutting feats, one rancher reported his horse's brilliance, figuratively, by saying, "He could cut the baking powder out of a biscuit without breaking the crust."

HUMAN TRAITS

Possibly it was, in part, the human quality in horses —in this vast, lonely, unsettled country—that drew men and horses together in a peculiarly intimate fashion. Horses and men seemingly complemented one another's nature in the wild country.

Horses are gregarious animals. They need company. Otherwise they become nervous and develop strange fears. On the Plains, during wild-horse days, a solitary mustang seemed always to be seeking company. A man-driven *remuda* was sometimes joined by a lone stallion—presumably whipped from his band or unable to assemble one. A lone horse was an unhappy, frustrated animal. When no other company was available or compatible, they often took up with buffaloes or elks.[15]

A frightened bunch of mustangs would usually run toward any other animals in sight—buffaloes, antelopes, wild cattle or another group of mustangs.

Like people, horses are creatures of habit. Left to their own designs and conveniences, they water at the same spot

★

day after day. Even if they wander far away, they will often pass satisfactory watering places and walk miles to drink at a certain favorite spot.[16] This habit led to many wild horses being captured at, or near, their favorite watering places.

A range mare usually drops her colt year after year in the same place. Frontiersmen of pre-fence days, who drove herds of horses long distances told of many instances in which mares traveled hundreds of miles in the spring to get back to their stamping grounds to have their colts.

Mustangers learned that superstition and curiosity are very pronounced in horses. Plowed furrows angled out from a pen gate could be as effective as wing fences. Wild horses feared a black line of unsodded earth, whereas wire fences usually were ineffective with wild horses. But if the wires were draped with white rags the animals would shy away. One mustanger made effective pens and wings out of bolts of canvas fastened onto pickets. A saddle blanket or large sack hung up at a watering place would, for a time, cause wild horses to avoid it.[17] Many horses have refused to cross a railroad track.

Stallions like to advertise, to stake claim to their desired range. Early travelers on the Plains found huge piles of freshly topped manure—sign of mustang country. Each day, the stallion added to his private heap as a notice to other stallions that he had been there. Dung pyramids as high as eight feet have been found.

Possibly no animal has so personified the spirit of freedom as the horse. Running wild on the Plains, long mane and tail flying in the breeze, hoofs pounding the endless grasslands, he appeared a vivacious, joyous creature in the extreme. He fought captivity with tooth and hoof and every fiber of his freedom-loving body. Only a small percentage of wild horses on which the attempt was made were tamed. Even a domesticated horse, once it had a chance to run free with a wild bunch, seldom missed the opportunity.

According to numerous reports, it usually took more time to tame a horse, than for one to go wild, if he escaped to freedom. One observer stated that the gentlest plowhorse that took up with a wild band would in two days become as wild as the wildest of the lot.

Many old-timers say that many horses committed suicide rather than give up their freedom. Even though submitting to the saddle, many of them lost the instinct for life. Captivity broke their spirit forever. One frontiersman told of riding a tamed horse into water to drink. The animal pushed his muzzle into the water up to his eyes. Then he lay down. Three men struggled to pull his nose out of the water, but he would not yield. He drowned on the spot.[18]

In numerous instances mustangers, after dogging a bunch of mustangs for days, finally saw them plunge over a cliff to death to escape. One mustanger followed a bunch of 20 wild ponies until he finally penned them, only to find that 18 of them would not eat. They died in their prison without touching food.[19]

Horses suffer from fear much as people do. A trail driver wrote, "While the storm was in progress, the horses bunched together around me, stuck their heads between their knees and moaned and groaned . . . as though the end of time had come."

Renne Allred, a Texas rural mail carrier, bought a bay mare to pull his buggy; but when he hitched her up she

★

would not budge. When he whipped her, she stood almost perpendicular on her hind feet. She would not kick, but she refused to pull a pound. Allred had heard that a balky horse would sometimes pull by the tail. So he got some wire, made it fast to her tail, and tied it to the cross bar. She pulled the buggy with her tail satisfactorily. After a while he loosened her tail. Once primed in this fashion she worked satisfactorily for the day. The mail carrier drove her for years. He bragged that she was one of the fastest trotters and most reliable animals he ever knew; but every morning, to the very last day, she had to be started off pulling the buggy by her tail.[20]

A couple of Texas cowboys wanting to take their girl friends to a dance one night, found that there were no work horses to pull a wagon. So they hitched their cow ponies to it. The ponies refused to tighten the traces. Every type of persuasion failed. Finally, one of the cowboys got out and mounted one of the ponies bareback and started riding him that way. Traveling proceeded orderly; but the cowboy did not get to ride beside his girl any of the distance. When he got off his pony, the power was off until he mounted again.[21]

Horses are very susceptible to odors. They have been known to show reaction of pleasure or displeasure to perfumes worn by lady riders. Experienced wild-horse tamers avoided altering their odor by change of clothes, especially their underwear, while following mustangs and trying to get them accustomed to them. Some mustangers, after penning the animals, would walk around the fence several times to accustom the horses to their odor before entering the pen.

Usually, whatever a determined horse put his mind to

he accomplished, whether to satisfy his master or rid himself of him. The stubbornness of both rider and mount is well illustrated by Rollins: "The shock of bucking was so severe that many a rider bled from the nose, the mouth, sometimes the ears; not a few men fainted in the saddle. . . . Many men were ruptured, and in very rare instances men fell dead from their animals' backs. An autopsy upon the body of a rider who had thus died, disclosed a liver entirely torn from its moorings." [22] One Negro rider was pitched to death by a bad horse, but was never thrown.[23] Rollins stated that about one horse in 500 was an outlaw that could never be broken, and about one in 10,000 was a "man-killer." [24]

A trail driver told of a stubborn horse he used on the trail that had to be taken across the streams on a ferry boat. He refused to try to swim. In the water, "he would only turn upon his side, curl up his tail, and float back to the bank."

One rancher had a valuable horse that made bridling an exhausting task. One day he chanced to saddle the horse before trying to bridle him. Much to his surprise the horse accepted the bit without the slightest protest. After that, he always saddled him before bridling and had no further trouble.[25] It was surmised that he had been broken that way, but there is no way of knowing. It is as difficult to explain the eccentricities of horses as it is those of people.

EQUINE MARVELS

Extraordinary feats in the Old West often concerned horses; and in the quiet of the day, when men's legs were relaxing from the bow of the saddle, they boasted, and fought, and made plans about horses.

★

Even as an old man, Ad. Lawrence loved horses as few men have. Whenever there was talk of good horses, he always told the sad and wonderful story of his favorite black mare, and it was with a tenderness that men reserve only for favorite women or favorite horses.

One summer day in 1832 Lawrence and some companions went on a mustang hunt on the prairie near the Trinity River. In time, they discovered a herd of about 100 mustangs. As they approached, the animals showed no signs of fear. The men were noting this strange circumstance when the long grass of the prairie suddenly became alive with Indians, one for each horse. The savages mounted their ponies with a jump and made for the whites at full speed.

The men turned tail and headed for the nearest settlement ten miles away. They were on good mounts, but Ad. Lawrence's black mare was, according to his statement, "a little ahead of anything in that country for speed and bottom."

The Texans gained some on the Indians the first three miles, but their horses began to tire. The Indians divided, forming columns to the right and to the left. The reason soon became apparent. There was a deep ravine ahead that could not be crossed. To head the ravine, the men had to ride into the column to the left.

Lawrence reached the head of the ravine, ahead of his companions, the yelling savages a bare 100 yards behind. He gave his mare the reins, touched her with the spurs, and turned the corner. Arrows were flying thick in the air. One stuck in his buckskin jacket and another in his mare's neck. The black mare spurted straight away and made a slight gain. Lawrence looked back for his companions. All were down. About half the Indians had stopped to scalp the Texan, but the others were dashing toward him without any letup.

Lawrence could see the timber along the Trinity three miles away. If he could get a few yards more margin and hold it for three miles he might save his hair; but at this moment he became dizzy and began to wobble in the saddle. He dropped his rifle. It seemed that the end had come, for in such a race, one second could mean the difference between life and death.

The black mare, with a slack rein, lost no time. In a few moments Lawrence straightened up. He managed to pull the arrow out of the mare's neck. He noted now that she was blowing hard. At this point, he made a gamble and a sacrifice. His heavy leather coat with the arrow in it was flopping and catching a lot of wind. It was a protection against arrows, but his mount needed every advantage to win. He shucked off the coat and dropped it to the ground.

For another mile, Lawrence held his own; but the mare was blowing hard. Here Lawrence made another sacrifice for his mare—another long risk. He stopped to let her rest, though the prairie was swarming with Indians. He dismounted and loosened the saddle girth. One Indian was not more than 100 yards off.

With bridle reins in one hand and his hunting knife in the other, he waited for the lead Indian to come on. This stop would be declared foolish by many when Lawrence told the story—this stopping the race when ahead—but Ad. Lawrence, who knew horses like few people did,

★

would say that the best of horses can stand only so much. The lead Indian never stopped until he was within a few steps of Lawrence. He was so sure of a kill that he threw away his bow and charged with a long knife. As Lawrence told it, "he ran full against my knife, and I left him lying there."

Lawrence took off his boots to lighten the mare's load, tightened the girth, and mounted. Arrows began falling about him, but every jump of his mare was bringing him closer to the timber of the Trinity.

He reached the timber safely, but he was yet far from saved. Bluffs 15 to 20 feet high formed the river bank. The Indians were crowding close. Either horse and man had to go over together or Lawrence had to go alone.

The mare stopped short at the edge of the bluff, drew back and snorted; but hearing the yells of the Indians close behind, she plunged over. Man and animal sank deeply into the water from the high dive; but the mare rose, with Lawrence still in the saddle, and headed for the opposite bank.

Safety appeared only a matter of seconds away; but two-thirds across the river the mare gave a groan, quivered a moment, and sank from under the rider. Lawrence swam to the nearby bank, and was safe. Not a single Indian dared take the leap into the river.[26]

ENDEARING NAMES

Texans have never been more imaginative than when naming their horses. Sometimes a name was determined by a characteristic of the animal, or some unusual circumstance associated with it; often, it expressed an attitude of devotion or contempt.

J. Frank Dobie tells of a horse named "Kerosene." While still a young, long-haired filly, she was roped to be branded. She was found to be covered with ticks and was rubbed with kerosene to kill the insects. Then the hot branding iron was applied. She instantly burst into a blaze, broke loose from the men and rushed into the *manada* a fiery streak. Fortunately, she was roped quickly, thrown to the ground and the flame smothered with dirt. Though badly scorched, the filly recovered, but ever afterward she had white spots all over her, and was always called "Kerosene." [27]

Texas Ranger Jesus Sandoval owned an odd but appropriately named horse.[28] Sandoval was a prosperous Mexican whose stock was stolen, house burned, and family violated by Mexican raiders. It is said that he joined the Rangers for protection and better opportunities for revenge. He became official hangman for the Rangers.

A fellow Ranger described his system thus: "Casuse (Jesus) would make a regular hangman's knot and place the hangman's loop over the bandit's head, throw the end of the rope over the limb, make the bandit get on Casuse's old paint horse and stand up in the saddle. He would make the loose end fast, get behind the horse, hit him a hard lick and the horse would jump under the spy, breaking his neck instantly." His paint horse logically became known as "Old Trapdoor."

"What Next" was buried beneath this epithet:

> He had the Body of a Horse,
> The Spirit of a Knight, and
> The Devotion of the Man
> Who Erected this Stone.[29]

★

Tom Smith, famed marshal of Abilene, realized that among cattlemen, particularly the spreeing trail drivers from Texas, nothing made a better and quicker impression than a fine mount. He patrolled the street of the wild cow town astride one of the best horses on the frontier, and, it was generally agreed, he commanded more respect than if he had been on foot. His horse bore the impressive name, "Silverheels." [30]

"Pretty Bloomers" was the name of a famous rodeo horse, which, thought to be relatively tame, had been bought for a lady bronc buster to ride. As soon as the rider came out of the shoot on him, he did about everything a bucking horse could do. Frank M. King told of the affair in his inimitable way: "As they romped past the grandstand, the little girl left the deck and as she flew off, head first, the band of her bloomers caught on the horn of the saddle, where she left 'em, and the hoss ran off around the arena with a pretty pair of red bloomers flying in the breeze, while the little lady rider landed in front of the grandstand with little more on her pretty form than what nature provided her with." A kid in the grandstand yelled: "Look at the pretty bloomers on the cow pony." [31] And the horse had the name "Pretty Bloomers" from then on.

A Texas pioneer popularly known as "Uncle Seth" had a rugged horse that he claimed had saved his scalp several times by keeping it a safe distance ahead of yelling Indians. He called his mount "Roarer." [32]

Another pioneer possessed a half-breed horse about which he bragged that "all the Indians in the Comanche nation couldn't catch me on him." He was aptly dubbed "Gitout." [33]

The C. C. Slaughter outfit had two horses with abilities as outstanding as their names. It was claimed that they could cut cattle without a bridle. They were named "Old Pompy" and "S. B."

The story is told that Buffalo Bill, after he had killed 4,283 buffaloes in the summer of 1869, named his buffalo horse "Brigham." [34]

Andy Adams possessed a hardy black horse that was a good swimmer and extremely valuable as a night horse to which he gave the name "Nigger Boy." [35]

Alfred Lane, on the Panhandle, had a big iron-gray horse that had been stolen by the Indians several times, and each time escaped and came back home. His name was "Drive." [36]

Fortunately for outlaws, horses never seem to loose their devotion to a master because of his morals. "Wild" Dick Yeager had a horse named "Cyclone" on which he outran many sheriffs and marshals. Finally, he was wounded in flight. The following day, a posse saw his horse in a corn field standing quietly with his head dropped. The posse found Wild Dick dead. Cyclone had stood all night and part of a day in the exact spot he was in when his master had dismounted and dropped the reins to the ground.[37]

The horse on which the outlaw, Lee Sage, outdistanced many peace officers was appropriately called "High Power." [38]

The eccentric and highly imaginative sculptress, Elizabeth Ney, had an oversized, "amicable, but slightly dim-witted" gig horse, which she named "Pasha" (The Passover).[39]

The naturalist, Jacob Boll, lived in Dallas; but much of his time was spent wandering over the lonely stretches of Texas on a little yellow pony appropriately called "Gypsy." [40]

John Neely Bryan, "the father of Dallas," rode across the country to the city's site on an Indian pony named "Walking Wolf." [41]

"Straightedge" was the name of Peckerwood Pete's horse, from which he roped the first locomotive he ever saw.

Ranger Captain D. W. Roberts owned a solid horse of such notable endurance in trailing outlaws that he called him "Old Rock." [42]

George W. Kendall, founder of the *New Orleans Picayune,* bought a horse in Texas to ride on the famous Santa Fé expedition. He was a heavy, powerful horse, "far from being a good horse to look at." Though already named when Kendall bought him, his appellation seemed in harmony with the ill-fated expedition. His name was "Jim the Butcher." [43]

COUNTRY COUSINS

The mule did not enjoy the dignified and beloved standing that the horse did; but he played an important part in frontier development. As hardy and tough as the untamed country, he seemingly had a down-to-earth intuition about the problems of the vast bewildering spaces. The burro, for instance, could travel where few beasts of burden or machines could. He could subsist on nature's stingiest offerings, and was a plodder able to endure with patience the most harsh and violent ravages of the elements.

The mule has not been used generally for a saddle animal. Most riders considered him slower, clumsier, and rougher than a horse. Usually, the feeling has been mutual—the mule did not care for the saddle, and he often found ways of excusing himself from this undesirable work, once he set his determined mind against it. "In violence of pitching motion, the mule outdid the horse" according to Rollins. "The average pitching bronco emitted grunts and snorts, and usually loud 'bawls' of rage, while a bucking mule rarely forgot to bray." [44]

The mule's alertness and endurance has usually been underestimated. John Young said: "Sometimes we might get a cross-run on a bunch of mustangs and cut or rope the saddle horses out, but we never caught a mule. A mule that had taken up with mustangs was always alert, ready to 'whistle' when he saw a man. One could never slip up on a bunch of mustangs that contained a mule, and the mule never tired on a run." [45]

Young told of an attempt to catch mustangs with a "mule playing in front as usual. Then he [the mule] decided to turn back; so he just high-tailed himself around me, the mustangs following. I headed them right again, but again the mule led them back. He had his mind made up . . . I discovered that he, rather than the stallion, was going to manage the mustangs that day. . . . He was the most valuable animal in the lot; but after a while, I realized that I could do nothing with the bunch so long as he was around. I shot him dead. Immediately the mustangs were under control again." [46]

"Outlaws" among mules are about as rare as among horses; but many stockmen contend that an outlaw mule is more difficult to handle, is more dangerous, and is less

★

likely to be subdued for useful purposes. Oran Warder Nolen tells of a mule saddled "while it was jumping, pulling, snorting, fighting." The bridle reins were placed over the mule's head, then the prospective rider took hold of the reins near the bits, preparatory to mounting. At that moment, "the mule swung his head viciously around, caught him by the wrist with its teeth and started running off, dragging the helpless man by the wrist, which was instantly broken when the animal seized him." [47]

THE SMART JACKASS

Ironically, the donkey possibly holds the world's record for withstanding stimulation. Once he balks or sulks, you can beat him, twist his anatomy into kinks, smother him, or even build a fire under him without results. All of which argues the point that if there is any animal on this earth with a mind of his own it is the donkey. Actually, with proper inspiration, he can be an ingenious creature. The old-timers, especially the mountain men, had considerable respect for the donkey.

Some claimed that a burro is so smart he acts dumb to get out of monotonous work. Certainly, he is one of the world's supreme hide-and-seek artists. A burro can stand stone still for hours perfectly camouflaging himself against a background of rocks and soil and shrubbery. One old weather-beaten prospector said: "I have spent 40 years camping and hunting in the hills . . . and it has taken 20 of these 40 years to locate my strayed burros." [48]

The donkey may not be as clever and hardy at securing food as the proverbial goat that eats tin cans. The donkey will not eat the can but he will gnaw the label off it. There is an account of a chuck wagon raided by a bunch of wild burros. They tore open everything, kicked the flour box to pieces and ate the contents, ate slabs of bacon, and pawed open canned peaches and licked up the juice.[49]

Because a burro may stand on three legs in the sun for hours at a time without apparent movement, does not mean that his big head is hollow, or his energy gone. This dozing laggard can, in a split second become a fireball of vicious energy. Once his mulish temper is aroused, his security or dignity threatened, he is an ingenious fighter. Actually, nothing on this continent can whip him.

If attacked by a wild beast, a horse will stand on his feet, unable to see accurately the assault on his rear; and, unable to put up an effective defense, may be rendered helpless by getting his hamstrings cut; or, if pounced upon at the neck, is unable to loosen his foe. When attacked by a panther, a burro has been seen to roll over on his back in such a position that he could see every point of his field of operation, kicking viciously and effectively, and with a noise that would terrify the boldest panther.[50] With no legs thus needed for standing purposes, tendon snapping wolves cannot find a temporarily stationary leg to get at. A wolf hit with a solid burro kick may as well be struck by lightning. This fighting position protects the burro's otherwise vulnerable neck.

A burro makes the best of neck animals for wild horses and cattle. Tie an untamed animal to his neck, and it is well taken care of. A burro, once he sets his head to it, takes no foolishness from man or beast. An unruly beast, thus yoked to him, may as well come along peacefully.

★

The burro will decide when to drink and when to graze, and the sooner the captive finds this out, the better it is for him. This may be fun for a burro, but it is not the lasting kind; and he is smart enough to know that the sooner he gets his unwilling teammate to the corral, the quicker his job is over. Thus, he usually attends to this duty with dispatch.

James A. McKenna told of a baby girl who followed a band of burros off from a mining town. The child's absence was not discovered until nearly dark. The howling of wolves could be heard. The townspeople organized and hunted frantically all through the night. It was not until sunrise that any trace was found. A bedding ground of the burros was found, also the baby's footprints.

The searchers were able to reconstruct the events of the past night. From all appearances, the animals had bedded down and the child had lain down about 30 feet away. Apparently, the herd had been startled by an attack, had turned back and hustled the child among them. There were several spots bearing signs of furious battle—wolf tracks mixed with those of the burros. Two big jacks must have done considerable kicking and biting, for at every place where a circle had been formed by the burros, with the child, the colts, and the jennies in the center, the searchers found blood, hair and bits of flesh.

Following the trail, the searchers observed that one of the jacks was bleeding and limping. They saw two wolves on the crest of a ridge. One limped badly.

They found the child unhurt. She said: "Oh, Mamma! The burros ran around me all the time." Her story collaborated in detail the belief the searchers gained from the signs.[51]

Old-timers contend that there is nothing wrong with the donkey's I. Q., that he is just misunderstood. He needs a challenge to bring out the best in him, they say.

★

Home on the Range

From the time Francisco Vasquez de Coronado drove his herd of cattle northward into Texas in 1540, Texas has been a cattle country. This stock, with various added mixtures, and the wild, limitless, rough country, with apparently every advantage and every evil, developed two of the toughest breeds known on this continent —the Texas longhorn and the hard-riding, hell-for-leather, Texas cowboy. Both are rapidly fading into legend; but they put on a grand, hilarious, adventurous show while they lasted—one that the world will doubtless read about for centuries to come. The two had much in common that the present-day, regimented, socialized citizens yearn for helplessly. The cowboy and the longhorn were the incarnation of rugged individualism.

THE COWBOY TRADITION

The western cattle country produced no dictators. Yet the cowboy was loyal to his boss. Those six-shooters and rifles he rode with on the range were not mere ornaments. He was a law unto himself and his clan. It was a rugged, harsh sort of law; but it carried respect because it was backed by the integrity of the individual.

The pistol was a symbol of consideration. One had to be considerate of a man carrying two handy six-shooters. The cowboy was not a polished individual; but he was sincere and as thoughtful and considerate of the feelings of others as he knew how to be. A woman was safe with him as long as she acted the lady. No real cowboy ever willfully insulted a lady, or lost a chance to resent any insult offered to one by another.

The cowboy was modest. One day a cowhand in a railroad coach which was being robbed by supposedly ex-cowboy bandits, heard a woman exclaim: "I have four hundred dollars in my purse, and I can't afford to lose it; please tell me how I can hide it."

The cowboy replied instantly: "Shucks! Miss, stick it in your sock; them fellers has nerve enough to hold up a train an' kill any feller that puts up a fight, but nary one o' them has nerve enough to go into a woman's sock after her bank roll!"

In the early days, locks at ranches were unknown. The unwritten law of the range decreed that any cattleman could use another's house, even if the owner was not present, for cooking and sleeping. The traveler took what he needed, but no more. The frontier cattleman could be depended upon to put the right brand on his neighbors' stock

71

★

at the roundup; he picked up strays on the long drives to market, and brought or sent the money to the owners. In the cattle country, there was no compromise with honesty; a man was on one side or the other—completely.

In time, some cowhands, through circumstance of Civil War range wars, and choice, turned outlaw; but even crime had a different complexion in those days. Reckless, daring men shot it out face to face. There are, however, virtually no records in early cattle land of sex crimes, kidnapping, or extortion. Men were bold, but at least they were not messy and vulgar with crime.

Cowboy regalia was symbolically a sign and a warning: "I can take care of myself, mister, just see that you recognize the fact and do the same for yourself!"

Badger Clark described "the Westerner" thus:

> I dream no dreams of a nurse-maid state
> That will spoon me out my food.
> A stout heart sings in the fray with fate
> And the shock and sweat are good.

OUTWITTING THE COW-BRUTE—SOMETIMES

A cowboy had to be tough and ingenious to handle the longhorns. Many cattlemen got their start capturing wild cattle. This was particularly difficult in the brush country, where the wary old longhorns would lay up in the brush all day and venture out only at night. It took patience and courage to capture these wild animals. Will James, in *Lone Cowboy*, wrote of this work: "Some was shot, quartered and packed out; others was trapped into stockades," in which blocks of salt had been placed. "A couple of riders would hide down in a pit by the heavy gate," and if and when a bunch came for the salt, the heavy gate was swung closed "mighty fast." "I've seen some of the heavy stockade corrals go down as if they was toothpicks when the wild bunch spooked and went against it." [1]

Capturing a longhorn was difficult, but this was only the beginning. Taming him took considerable time and know-how. A longhorn might be stupid, but what few ideas he had he held onto with a stubbornness known only to the bovine breed.

Cattlemen employed novel methods to subdue these wild animals. Sometimes they held captives on the spot, while other cattle were rounded up by sewing their eyelids shut with a needle and thread. The animal, unable to see, would not travel. When the herd was brought up, the captive could then be placed among the gentler cattle and the stitches removed from the eyelids. [2]

When wild animals continually tried to break loose from the herd on drives, cattlemen, as an extreme measure, cut a certain tendon in one of the animal's legs. This permitted the animal to walk, but it could not run. If it attempted to run, the leg would go limp and merely swing back and forth, causing it to fall. [3]

Tenderness was not an instinct to be encouraged in handling longhorns. Fighting troublemakers were sometimes subdued by shooting them through the thick part of their horns with a six-shooter. The jar caused by a center shot would immediately take a steer's mind off fighting. If the pith was punctured the soreness usually lingered long

★

enough to make him manageable for weeks. At times, tired, disgusted cowboys did not bother very much about taking careful aim. If they shot a little lower than the horn, they considered the "accident" good riddance. One outlaw could spoil a whole herd of cattle. They had to be subdued or killed.[4]

Next to a brute that runs too much, the most exasperating is one that will not run at all. Seemingly, there is no standard remedy for a sulled ox. What will make one tear a barn down taking off seems to lull another to sleep. Some prescribed remedies (I've seen most of these and many others fail at times): twist the tail, stuff nostrils with snow; pour half a box of snuff in each nostril; sick the dogs on the beast; hold nostril and mouth closed to stop breathing, etc.

Cattle normally will not swim a large stream facing the sun. One explanation is that cattle refuse to start swimming when they cannot see a landing on the other side. This does not appear to be a satisfactory answer; but there is no need for any mortal to apologize for not knowing what a cow is thinking. If an experienced cattleman, driving west, came to a river in the late afternoon, he waited until morning to put the herd across.[5]

It often took ingenuity and courage to put a herd across a stream, especially if it was swollen. Sometimes cattle jammed in streams like logs, for no explainable reason. W. B. Foster told of an experience in which "the cattle got about the middle of a stream and then went to swimming in a circle. . . . I stripped to my underclothes, mounted 'Jack Moore' and went to them. I got off the horse and right onto the cattle. They were so jammed together that it was like walking on a raft of logs. When I finally got to the only real big steer in the bunch, I mounted him and he pulled for the other side. When he got near the bank, I drifted down the stream to my horse." [6]

TRAIL DRIVERS

One of the big problems of the Texas cattlemen was getting their stock to the distant markets. Transportation was definitely by way of hoofs.

On the first drive, the cattlemen carried food and equipment on pack horses across the endless prairie, mountains, and rivers. This bundlesome inconvenience, in time, suggested the chuck wagon, with its hinged end-gate as a cook's work table, the sour-dough jar, etc.

Often, a herd of several thousand head had to be counted—at the start of the drive, or after a stampede or a mixup with another herd. An experienced cowboy could sit in the saddle in a fog of dust and flies and count, ac-

★

curately, several thousand steers. To do this, the herd was strung out as thinly as possible. The cowboy tallied his count by tying a knot in a saddle string for each 100 head. Two cowboys often worked together, one on either side of the line of cattle. At the tying of each knot, each called to the other to check the accuracy of his count.

One of the big problems, especially on the long drives across the plains, was fuel for cooking and, at times, for warmth. Most chuck wagons carried an old cowhide suspended under it called the "caboose," into which were thrown stray pieces of wood, as long as the outfit traveled in wooded country.

Often the drives had to depend upon finding old bedding grounds in order to secure cow chips for a campfire. This was not always easy, for many of the old trails were dim and overgrown with grass.

The drivers sometimes had fuel to "sell." The drivers frequently needed a pen to hold the cattle at night; just a fence on one side would be a great aid in holding the stock when restless. The nesters also were usually hard-pressed for fuel, and would bargain with the drivers to use their pen or fences in order to get the fuel left on the bedding grounds.[7] On occasion, the drivers used the fine wood of rat dens for firewood.

Water was an almost constant problem—too much or too little. There are accounts of drives going 96 hours and longer without water. Cattle often died of thirst, killed themselves plunging over bluffs after water, or piled into streams crushing or drowning others in their mad rush for water.

Sometimes, after reaching a stream, the water was not

safe for men to drink. In such instances, the cowboys frequently dug shallow holes near the stream and let the water seep into them for use. Muddy water could be settled by dropping a peeled prickly pear into it.

At times, cowboys got too much water in the wrong form. Hail was a menace. Often it poured down upon them in large enough forms to peel heads and stampede the stock. But cowboys learned how to turn disadvantages into a good thing. When it was over, they often scooped up the ice, dumped it into the water barrel and had the treat of ice water in summer.

When crossing streams, cowboys frequently swam with the herd. When tired, one might catch a big steer by the tail or straddle him; and the animal would take him to the bank in a hurry.[8]

Dangerous quicksand lined the edges of many streams. Nothing exasperated a cowboy like a cow bogged down in quicksand. Hundreds were abandoned on the drives hopelessly bogged. Frank M. King told how he overcame a quicksand problem: "A bunch of us would ride our horses back and forth to sorta pack the sands; and then we would run a bunch of loose horses over and back a few times." Then the cattle were driven over safely. King explained, "A horse will pick up his feet and move quick when he feels it sinking; but a steer will stop to see what's up, and while he hesitates he is lost."[9]

Some fiction writers have given the impression that whisky was the big drinking problem on the drives. If the men carried whisky at the beginning, it did not last long, and for months they usually had no opportunity to buy a drink. Coffee was the choice drink. Trail bosses

★

realized the urgent need of this beverage for men who worked long, monotonous hours, many of them at night.

The bosses had to bear in mind that these sleepy, touchy cowboys wore side arms; therefore ingenious methods were devised to provide substitutes when the real coffee ran out. Sometimes the cooks ground and parched corn or okra. Such substitutes might not fool the cowboys, but were much better than nothing and usually kept them reasonably satisfied for a short time. Coffee was not always sufficient to keep the boys awake during the long night hours. At times, they resorted to putting tobacco into their eyes to stay awake.

It took a lot of tricks to outwit the Indians. Joe S. Clark outsmarted the Indians once on a return trip. He saw many bands of Indians every day and could see their signals—smoke by day and fires at night. They did not attempt to attack him in the daytime, "so we would camp early in the evening and allow the mules to rest; then, as soon as darkness enveloped us, we would hitch up and drive 10 or 15 miles and camp without making a fire." [10]

STAMPEDES

Stampedes were a constant threat. No one ever found any insurance against stampedes; but calmness or excitability in men influenced cattle in like manner. For that reason, cowboys when on guard at night often sang, strummed a guitar, or played a harmonica trying to keep the herd convinced that all was well. Some men claimed that hanging lanterns near the bedded herd helped. The men learned to exert every effort to keep away anything exciting.

Possibly nothing was more dangerously exciting than a cattle stampede—wild longhorns thundering in savage madness over plains, gullies, cliffs; with yelling, cursing cowboys riding pell-mell through pitch darkness, rain, hail, and lightning trying to prevent them from scattering to the four winds.

A stampede was about the easiest and quickest thing to start known to cowmen. J. Frank Dobie, in *A Vaquero of the Brush Country*, wrote: "Sometimes, when cattle stampede, they stampede from a reclining position—one jump to their feet and the second jump to hell." [11] Goodnight, who understood cattle about as well as anyone, admitted that their actions were almost impossible to predict. He wrote: "Often 3,000 steers have been dozing in peace. . . . Then 'something happened,' and with unbelievable suddenness, as quick as the flash of a wakeful eye and as unexpected as the flash of a covey of hidden quail, with an unearthly roar that was the blending of innumerable hoofbeats, with the distinct quaking of the earth as if in fear itself, the cattle were up together and gone. . . . They flashed to their feet, apparently all headed in the same direction, and in impenetrable but perfectly coordinated mass, they stampeded." [12]

Half-asleep cowboys sprang upon their horses and dashed out to turn the herd. In "turning," the cowboys pushed the swift animals in front into a circle until they caught the tail of the long-strung, stampeding herd, and thus threw the cattle into a mill. Goodnight observed that cattle invariably circled to the right. He never heard of a bunch circling counter-clockwise. [13]

Men and cattle often were killed, and good horses

ruined for life. Racing after a panicky herd of cattle, where neither the ground nor the cattle could be seen, was considered the most nerve-racking experience of range life. Cowboys in early days were considered too great a risk for any life insurance company to insure.[14]

Cattle often dehorned themselves in the mad rush. Andrew J. Jones wrote of a herd stampeding inside a pen containing some cedar stumps. Seventeen killed themselves by running against the stumps.[15] Sometimes stampeding cattle crushed through the roofs of dugouts, playing havoc with the frontier homes.[16] The cowboy preacher, J. W. Anderson, told of a herd that ran against some Negro cabins with such force that the houses fell, and a family of Negroes was killed by the crash. Many of the steers were trampled to death.[17]

Fiction gives innumerable accounts of men being trampled to death under the hoofs of stampeding cattle. Yet, strange to say, I cannot recall a single account in factual literature. Richard Withers, an experienced trail driver, wrote: "I soon learned that steers will not run over a man when he is down under foot. They will run all around a fellow, but I have yet to hear of a man being run over by them." [18]

Falls and lightning were among the greatest hazards. Many cowmen believed that cattle tend to attract electricity, mainly because of the heat they create. L. B. Anderson stated that he saw on various occasions several head of cattle and horses killed by one bolt of lightning.[19] Goodnight wrote: "Animal heat seems to attract electricity, especially when the cattle are wet, and after a storm I have seen the faces of men riding with a herd look scorched, as if some furnace blast had blazed against them. . . . The odor given off by the clashing horns and hoofs was nearly over-powering." [20]

In fighting stampedes in rain, cowboys often pulled off their slickers in order to avoid heating the body and attracting electricity. Probably one reason trail drivers paid so much attention to storms was the fact that they caused so many stampedes. The two worst hazards of the cowboy often descended upon him at the same time—an electrical storm and a consequent stampede. The number of deaths among cowboys caused by lightning, as found in records, is almost unbelievable.

Often, when several herds in the same vicinity stampeded on the trails, it took a week or more to separate the herds.

I have made notes on scores of causes of stampedes, and am convinced that, at least back in the days when cattle had horns, and muscles in their rumps instead of tender, dollar steaks, there wasn't a known system for out-figuring them; they could be depended upon to run from almost anything, and to run a long way, in an incredible hurry.

Many herds stampeded without apparent cause. Many of the causes, however, were known. Wild creatures caused most stampedes. Wild hogs could set off a chain reaction of fright. Hogs would usually stampede for "less than nothing," and for a bunch of them to come charging across a bedding ground was more than any herd of long-horns could take lying down.

Sometimes even the timid rabbit on an innocent nocturnal journey would get lost in the labyrinth of a herd of steers obstructing his path, and before he finished bump-

★

ing around working himself through, he would start a rampage that would take a day's time to stop.

Fear was more contagious than any disease. It spread faster and more completely. A startled deer might jump up in front of the lead steer. One jump and a snort from the steer, and those next went wild, and with the rapidity of an electric current the panic spread through to the drags. Running buffaloes, or just the scent of them, often stampeded herds. Cattlemen observed that the scream of one panther often sounded like a hundred. Disturbance by such animals always posed a problem. The shot of a gun for killing the animals might alarm the herd; and, on the other hand, the scream of a panther was a sound no longhorn would listen to for long on his belly.

The wise trail driver examined the ground closely before bedding a herd down for the night. Samuel Dunn Houston bedded his herd one night "on the worst gopher holes I could have found." He and his boys spent most of the night riding as fast as they could.[21] L. B. Anderson camped one night at the edge of a wood. He failed to notice that the timber was filled with roosting prairie chickens, thousands of them. The next morning, the noise these chickens made in leaving was too loud and strange for any herd to endure. Anderson lost several hundred beeves in the resulting stampede.[22]

Indians developed ruses to stampede cattle. Sometimes they shot arrows into the herds. One Indian tied a red blanket to a wild horse and started him toward a drive. The device worked wonders for the Indian.

The elements often started stampedes. Thunder and lightning rated high on the list. Rushing water caused by cloudbursts sometimes threw stock into a panic. The rush of thirsty cattle for water often reached stampede proportions. They might tear down anything in their path. Indian villages have been destroyed in this manner.

Frightened horses running through a herd frequently started stampedes. Several cowboys of the W. F. Thompson outfit tied their horses to a rail fence one night, several broke loose and dragged the rails into the herd. After the hard riding that night, the men in this outfit always tied their mounts to something more secure than a rail in a fence.[23]

Carelessness has caused many stampedes: R. T. Mellard wrote of a trail herd in 1871 bothered by a stray cow that kept "bawling around" and trying to get into the herd. One of the boys chased her off to what he thought a safe distance to fire his pistol to scare her; but the night was so dark that he had wandered back to the edge of his own herd. His pistol report was a thousand times more effective than he intended. Instead of scaring one cow off, it set a thousand steers on their feet—running.[24] L. B. Anderson said that the worst stampede he ever witnessed was caused by the noise of one of the men "having some fun with a Negro boy."

Danger was not limited to cowboys and cattle, but near tragedy sometimes turned into a "show." Once L. B. Anderson and his crew were driving a herd of Mexican steers through a long lane. They met a man and woman on horseback. A few minutes later the cattle stampeded, turned around, and plunged back in the opposite direction. As the cattle and drivers raced down the lane, Anderson was greatly concerned for the woman, who was riding side-

★

ways according to the custom of the day. It seemed inevitable that she would be overtaken, but as cattlemen and cattle charged close to her, the urge for security overcame modesty, and "that woman suddenly swung herself astride the horse . . . and pulled off a race that beat anything I ever saw. She outdistanced everything in that herd and rode away safely." [25]

CALVES

On the first long cattle drives to the railheads, all calves born en route were killed or abandoned. There was no known practical way to avoid the practice. The calves could not keep up with the herd. The drive could not stop until they were old enough for travel, because in a herd of thousands, calf-birth was a nightly affair. Calves were the big nuisance of the drives. Even if they could have made the trip, they were worthless at the shipping pens. No one thought of butchering a newborn calf.

It was often troublesome to drive a cow away from her calf. Sometimes the mother would bawl all night and all day and become a stampede menace with her noise and restlessness. Sometimes cowboys necked a grieving mother to a steer to get her started up the trail again. Cowboys made every effort to drive a cow away from her calf the instant she was delivered of it. If they accomplished this before she had time to smell it or let it suck, she would not make any trouble.

No drive started with calves. Ike Pryor of San Antonio contracted for 1,000 cows in Mason County in 1873. When he went to receive them, he found that half of them had calves. He called the seller to task, stating that he had contracted for dry cows and wanted nothing else. The seller said he did not want calves either. So the calves were separated from the cows, and 500 of them killed and the veal fed to hogs.[26]

When calves came to have a cash value, Charles Goodnight may have been the first to salvage them on the trail. He had a special wagon built that would haul 30 or 40 calves. The calf-wagons followed the herd, and cowboys picked up the calves as they were dropped. At night they were turned out with their mothers. Then in the morning, after they walked until tired out, they were roped and put into the wagon. This system, however, was not as simple as expected. Some people claim that a cow can always recognize her calf by its bawl, but Goodnight said that a cow knows her calf only by scent. Considering the trouble he had with cows and calves before he perfected his system, he should have known whereof he spoke. The first few times he turned the calves out of the wagon a milling mass of trouble started. The calves had rubbed together and mixed their scents so that the cows could not tell their own. To solve the problem he put each calf in a sack, and numbered the sack so as to get it on the same calf every morning.[27]

Often, nesters followed the drives to pick up the calves. As a rule, the cowboys did not regard these people with favor, and often played pranks on them. One nester drove up to a herd about dusk and was met by a cowboy who claimed to be the boss. The cowboy made a deal with him, agreeing to let him have all the calves found next morning if he would stand guard. He put the nester on the first relief and let him stay on guard all night. The cowboys had a loud and long laugh next morning when the very astonished and chagrined nester discovered what he should have discovered the evening before—that the herd contained nothing but steers.[28]

BRANDS

Texas imagination has known no bounds when designing cattle brands. The first brand had a religious significance—three Catholic crosses. It was worn by the cattle brought to Texas by Coronado.

Frank Hatch ran the .45 brand because, as he explained it, all he had when he started the herd was a Colt .45, and he intended using it to defend his stock.[29]

Henry Wells used the letters HEL because "hell is so famous," he said. A popular story exists to the effect that the famed 6666 brand was so adopted because four sixes in a poker hand won the money to buy the ranch. It was said that the Bar MD stood for "money down on the bar" from cattle buyers.

W. A. Walton used the percent mark because he hoped to make a good percentage of profits from his herd.

Many brands were shortened names, or names in symbols. Richard Fiveash used 5ASH. Jenne Bell, of Margaret, used a bell. John Wiseman, of Kountze, fashioned an owl's face. Mrs. M. C. Fish, of Houston, designed a fish. Mrs. W. G. Pots, of Spur, adopted a teapot. William Sachse adopted SX because he pronounced his name that way.[30]

Some brands appeared to be a form of correspondence, or greeting. There is a yarn about the IC brand which states that the owner began finding cattle in his herd branded

ICU. The IC owner, believing that his brand had been changed, decided to do a little changing himself and get in a pointed notice to the owner of the ICU. He changed his brand to ICU2. Jim Myers, of Kountze, might be accused of shouting this sentiment. His brand was OICU.[31]

B. Williams, of Young County, seemingly sent greetings to his fellow cattlemen by putting HOW U on his cows. It could be taken as a most cordial greeting, for it ran most of the length of the animal—large HOW on the left side and a large U on the left hip.

Some designs were accidental. The Waggoner brand, for instance, is three reversed D's. This, and many other reversed letter brands, can be explained by the fact that the cowhand who forged the brand made perfect letters without it occurring to him that when put on a cow they would be turned around.

In the open cattle country, there is a saying that men cannot carve love sentiments on trees, so they "carve" them on cowhide.

Some cattle have been valentines on hoofs. Brand designs run the gamut of the imagination, especially in the use of hearts. Clarence McDougall, of Harper, adopted Cupid's Heart. J. E. Egger, of Ebony, labeled his stock with an arrow-pierced heart; cattle of the Millee spread, of Lubbock, carry a heart-over-heart design (Two Hearts). Other Texas heart brands are: My Heart, Cross Heart, Heart Strings, Standing Heart, Circle Heart, Double Heart, T Heart, Lazy Heart, Bar Heart, Diamond Heart, etc., etc.

One of the most romantically inspired brands was the LIL, especially designed for a beautiful girl named Lily

★

Plunkett. Lily came to Texas with her father about 1880. They settled on a ranch, and before long all the neighboring cowboys came under the spell of her charm.

Most cowboys were timid and awkward at flirtation, but many could work artistic wonders with a running iron. They wanted to show their affection for the pretty ranch girl, but the dainties of department and candy stores were foreign and unappealing to them. Nothing so appealed to them in the gift line as a pretty calf. So their method of courting her was to brand any maverick they could find and present it to her as a gift. LIL was appropriately chosen as a brand, and competition was so keen that soon Lily had a sizable herd of yearlings as fine as the best judgment of admiring cowboys could select.

It would be romantic to report that Lily married one of the cowboys who wooed her in such an imaginative and valuable way; but this is a true story, of realism—not a fairy tale. Lily wrote back East to her old boy friend and told him how easy it was to get a start in the cattle business out West. He came to Texas, married her, and ran the LIL herd into a fortune.[32]

The most fantastic brand in the Big Bend country was placed on a yearling at a roundup held north of Alpine in January, 1890. One of the larger outfits did not approve of the roundup but sent one of its men, Fine Gililland, over to look after its interest.

Among the mavericks was a brindle yearling. Some of the boys said they had seen it earlier that year following one of Poe's cows. Poe was called. He cut the calf out of the herd and started with it toward a group of his yearlings away from the main herd.

Gililland loped up to him and told him the calf did not belong to him.

Gililland cut it, and the two men chased the calf back and forth between their bunches. Both men tried to get their rope on the animal. It ran back into the main herd. Gililland came out with the yearling. Poe, now aggravated with an unruly horse and frightened calf, along with a man bent on taking what he thought was his yearling, decided to end the matter by shooting the yearling. He drew his six-shooter, fired, and missed. Gililland drew his gun and shot Poe dead.

Gililland, seeing what he had done, struck out for the Glass Mountains. He was killed a few weeks later in a gunfight with the Rangers.

After Poe's death, nobody at the roundup wanted to put his brand on a yearling that had caused a murder. The cowboys, still stunned by the fantastic turn of events, huddled on the outer rim of the herd in a conference. They reached a strange decision, and there followed one of the most eerie rituals possibly ever performed at a branding fire. The cowboys designed a new brand, never worn before or since, so far as is known. This, they calculated, would stop forever all arguments of ownership of the animal. They roped the yearling and pulled him up to the fire, and there with a running iron one of the men burned the letters MURDER deep into his hide. The brand in big letters stretched from shoulder to flank.

The animal became a legend. Nobody wanted him, nobody cared for him. It would seem from the legend that the other cattle of the range spurned him as if he were a cursed creature, for he wandered about the country alone

★

the rest of his life. He became a wild, elusive creature, and in his later days, it is said, only occasional glimpses were caught of him, usually at dusk. It was reported that he turned gray, all except his weird brand, which spelled out MURDER across his side in large, dull-red letters.[33]

★

CHAPTER FIVE

Food

During the days of the Republic, a newspaper commentator wrote: "The ill cooked, unwholesome food which is so often at our taverns is the fruitful source of disease. The heavy sodden dough balls . . . in the shape of 'hot rolls' should be shunned by a hungry traveler as he would shun a charge of grapeshot; indeed, we believe the grapeshot of the Mexicans have committed less havoc among our citizens than these vile dough balls." [1]

Corn was a staple on the frontier. Though tedious to prepare, this cereal could be made into delicacies "fit for a king." The Texas Ranger often prepared bread in the open in this fashion: "He took his corn and broke it as fine as he could between two flat stones, and then, with some fat, fried from the bacon, mixed a cake, which he baked, wrapped in green leaves, by a bed of ashes and hot coals in a hole in the grounds." [2] One man who tasted this bread said that he had "never eaten anything the memory of which was more delicious."

The colonists were not so adept in handling wheat flour.

91

One observer stated that many children "had never known what wheaten bread was like." A Mrs. Martin Varner made her first "batch of biscuits." After an attempt at eating the product, a young son took his biscuit and disappeared into the yard. In a short time he came back for another biscuit. Doubting the lad's ability to eat so quickly, the father went out to investigate. He found that the child had punched holes through the center of the biscuits, inserted a stick axle, and was playing "Mexican cart," with them.[3]

Texas Rangers knew that it was possible to live solely on a meat diet. Olmstead told of meeting a Ranger leader who said that he had been out with his men "six months from the settlements, with nothing to eat but game during that time."[4] All they wanted when they returned to civilization was to "eat some bread and vegetables; and they were ready to go out again." Six months in the woods was considered no feat at all for a Texas Ranger, as long as he had his rifle and kept his powder dry!

Settlers, as well as Rangers, usually ate a wide variety of game. Some men fancied panther meat; it was supposed to make hair grow on the chest. Here is a recipe for panther: "Cut a forked limb and thrust the forked point in a thick slice of meat, hold it over a hot, glowing fire, so that in five or ten minutes, at most, you have cooked both sides, and left it filled with rich juice which will ooze out of your bread while partaking it." [5]

COFFEE

If there is one thing Texans have always been sensitive about, it is the quality of the coffee they brew. Modern Texans talk about the poor coffee in restaurants as they talk about the weather and lament that nothing can be done about it.

Occasionally, a proprietor will blab out the straight facts. One woman restaurant owner in Dallas, when asked about the blend she served, replied: "Oh, I buy the cheapest coffee I can get at the A & P and boil hell out of it." [6]

But, good or bad, the average Texan has always insisted upon his cup of coffee—regardless, come war, famine, or poor cooks. W. S. Adair wrote of his father trading a farm for a sack of coffee during the scarcity caused by the Civil War. "He tried parched grain and acorns, and often got something that looked like coffee, but never anything with the Java kick to it. Toward the end of the war, Mexican smugglers slipped some across the Rio Grande, a few sacks

★

of which got as far as Sherman. Father traded his farm for one of the sacks and ran home with it, actually yelling with joy." [7]

The story is told of an old couple who had been married 50 years. The wife began reading "health hints" in the newspaper, and decided that coffee was injuring her husband's health. Day after day she tried to prevail upon him to give up the habit, but without success. Finally, one morning at breakfast she said: "Hank, if you don't quit drinking coffee, I'll leave you!"

He looked across the table in bewildered silence for a full minute and then replied: "Honey, I'm gonna miss you."

One could boil coffee, drip it, or percolate it, and serve it in a tin cup or a gourd, without sugar or cream, and keep a reputation; but one thing the coffee server had to do if he expected to hold his head up in society—he had to put in enough coffee. Frank M. King gave this recipe for making good coffee: "Put two pounds of coffee in one gallon of water; boil two hours, then throw a horseshoe into the pot and if it sinks the coffee ain't done." He said, "The trouble with most coffee makers is, they are too dern liberal with the water." [8]

TABLE CONVERSATION

Texans have been notably plain-spoken about their food. Table conversation, on the frontier, was often more picturesque than charming.

Range men liked their steaks well done. One cowboy, upon being served a rare steak in a restaurant, requested the waitress to take it back and cook it done.

"It's done," the waitress insisted.

"Lady," the cowboy said, "I've seen cows hurt worse than that and get well!"

If food became too fancy, cowboys thought up names for it. When one cowman's wife mingled fruit with red jello, the husband called it "train wreck." The first corn flakes on the range were called "skillet scabs," meringue on lemon pie was "calf slobber," rice pudding, "moonshine." One cowboy when faced with a dish of jello rejected it with the comment: "I'd as soon ride into a west wind with a funnel in my mouth." [9]

A rigid rule of the cow camp decreed that whoever complained about the chuck had to do the cooking. One cowhand who had a distressingly long run of cooking, due to the lack of a complaint, determined to rid himself of the job by throwing a handful of salt into the biscuit dough and then giving it the fast bake treatment.

At mealtime, one cowpoke burst out: "These biscuits are burned on the bottom and top, and raw in the middle, and salty as hell—" He hesitated a moment until he could control himself, and then added: "But they are shore fine, just the way I like 'em."

Two cowboys were eating a meal in a restaurant. One said: "The butter is so strong it could walk around the room and say hello to the coffee."

His pal took a sip of his coffee and said: "Well, if it did, the coffee is too weak to answer back."

C. L. Ford in *Parade of the Pioneers* tells of a visit Sam Houston made to his grandfather's house about dinnertime one day. The General said: "Now Mrs. Ford, don't you put yourself out one bit on my account; all I want is

★

plenty of good buttermilk and some corn pone with your fingerprints on it." [10]

Once at a dinner in his honor, Houston, while talking, lifted a big spoonful of hot rice pudding to his mouth. Breaking a sentence in the middle, he spat the fiery mouthful onto the table. Probably he came about as near as it is possible to turn bad manners into a matter of enviable judgment, when he said dryly: "A lot of durn fools would have swallowed that."

★

CHAPTER SIX

Entertainment, Strictly Homemade

One mark of a true frontiersman was his ability to enjoy a hearty laugh, whether at his own or someone else's expense. Laughter was the great escape valve for men of taut nerves, struggling against the elements, hostile Indians, and outlaws on a lonely frontier. Though the frontiersmen were usually busy trying to tame the wilderness and bring some comforts into hardships, time often hung heavily on their hands.

The pioneers had to make almost everything they had, including entertainment. That the rugged Texans produced a pungent, sometimes crude, brand is not surprising.

The captive survivors of the Mier Expedition were forced under guard to build roads in Mexico. When carrying dirt or pebbles in sacks, the Texans often tore a hole

★

in the sack which let the load drip out, and by the time the carriers arrived at their destination, there frequently was not "enough material left in the sack to make a dirt-dauber's nest."

Big Foot Wallace told how some of the stoutest men were hitched to carts and worked like horses. One prisoner decided that if he had to be geared up and worked like a horse, he would act like one. So while the carts were traveling slowly along the edge of an embankment he suddenly pretended to take fright at some object, and giving a snort "that a mustang wouldn't have been ashamed of," he dashed away with his cart and no amount of hollering would stop the runaway. Finally, he stopped at a distance, and in Texas bronco fashion, kicked over the traces; and to leave nothing undone in the horse act, kicked the cart over the precipice where it was dashed to pieces on the rocks below.

Wallace stated that he believed the Mexicans thought it was "one of the natural characteristics of the 'wild Texans' to stampede occasionally like wild horses." Instead of punishing him, the Mexican enjoyed a big laugh along with the Texans. The man-horse was given a shovel and never harnessed again.[1]

Even in the military service, under orders, the average trooper usually found opportunity for his own particular brand of fun. James P. Gorman, of the Bastrop community, was wagon master in General Rusk's Army, but he was just a frolicking boy at heart. The general sent him to Linn's Landing on the bay to bring in a cannon that had been landed there.

From the first sight of the field piece, Gorman was eager

to test its merits. En route back, he saw a drove of deer grazing in the distance. What he did probably is unique in hunting annals: Soldier Gorman went deer hunting with a cannon. He maneuvered into position, put in a charge of grape, aimed the cannon and set it off. He failed to bag a single animal, but the boom of the cannon brought General Rusk with a detachment to him post haste. It was supposed that he had engaged the enemy.

The general placed Gorman under arrest; but Gorman swore "the show was worth it." He had never had so much fun in his life. "My range was a little short," he related, "but you ought to have seen those deer go in the air when the shot cut the dust under their feet." [2]

Almost anything might happen to a greenhorn on the cattle range. When an uninitiated cowboy showed up at a ranch seeking work—and a horse to work on—he quite likely would be assigned his first job herding antelope. He would not need a horse herding antelope, because they were afraid of a man on a horse. Thus, many a tenderfoot was started across the plains on a 10 or 15 mile hike to round-up antelope.

Greenhorns, without proper frontier courage, were often made miserable and kept close to the campfire after dark by frightful stories of "gwinders," extremely vicious animals with one short leg in front and one behind, so arranged that they could circle quickly around a mountain and catch a man and tear him to pieces.

One greenhorn moved into a West Texas community, bought a herd of cattle and drove them to his ranch. A group of neighboring cowboys gathered around his cowpen, and began laughing at his cattle.

★

"What's the matter?" the newcomer demanded.

"I really hate to tell you," one of the boys said. "But you got a bunch of old run-down stock loaded off on you. Those cattle haven't got any front teeth in the upper jaw." The more the boys laughed the angrier the greenhorn became. But to help out, the boys agreed to help him drive the cattle back to the original owner to get his money back. Everybody involved lost about a day's work, but all considered the show worth the price—just to see the color of this tenderfoot's face when told that adult cattle do not have front teeth in the upper jaw.[3]

On the long cattle drives to the northern markets, when for months on end, cowboys had only cowboys and cows for company, time often passed tediously slow. What amusement they enjoyed they had to devise. On one of the drives in 1871, a colonel with long white hair who had a way of "putting things over on the boys" was bossing one of the outfits. One evening the boys set the colonel's tent up over a bed of polecats. And when the colonel went to bed they tied the flaps of his tent . . . You guessed it. The colonel tore the tent down.[4]

Gus Black told how he furnished some fun and consternation for his men on a drive. One morning he found a couple of long horns that had slipped off the head of a dead cow on the trail. He fitted them onto the just-sprouting horns of a runty dogie among the drags.

Sometimes horseplay was definitely for the horse. John Young related how he got rid of a stray horse. This stray was a nuisance stamping about his corral. So, late one afternoon he roped and blindfolded him and tied to his tail a dried beef hide that happened to be hanging on the fence, and turned him loose. It would all have been good, hilarious fun solely at the horse's expense, but Young's partner happened at this moment to be just out of sight driving a *remuda* to the corral. The stray headed straight into the *remuda*, and dried beef hide sailing behind like a kite on a short string, and the frantic horse snorting wildly and knocking up the turf at every jump. The *remuda* scattered over a ten-mile section of country, and it took a week to round it up. A good deal of cursing and threatening was done before Young's partner could laugh at this one.[5]

Even officers, on the serious business of facing death to preserve the peace, had to be able to take a joke. J. Evetts Haley, in his biography of Jeff Milton, tells about Milton in the tough town of Colorado City. Orders had been issued for all cowboys to check their guns upon arriving in town. One day as Jeff was passing a saloon, a patron came out stating that a riled man in there was saying "no damn Ranger was going to take a pistol off him." Then another customer came out and warned the Ranger. "Don't go in. A man in there said he'll kill anybody that tries to take his gun. And he's got his gang with him."

Jeff Milton was too brave and efficient a Ranger to ignore such a challenge. He stepped in, noted a man standing at the bar with his back to the door, with a conspicuous bulge in his coat, obviously made by the handle of a six-shooter. He was repeating: "I'd like to see the man that can take a pistol off me."

At that moment Milton, with his gun drawn, said: "I'll take it." And he did. But what he took was a sawed-off plow handle. The house shook from the roar of laughter, and the Ranger bought the drinks for the crowd.[6]

Jeff could dish them out as well as take them; but there

★

was one firm, exacting Ranger, Adjutant General John B. Jones, who could not, and Jeff knew it. That was an unendurable challenge.

While fishing one day, a rancher came along and asked Jeff where he got his fish hooks. He said he had been trying to buy some. "I bought them from the little Jew up there in the tent," Jeff said, pointing toward the adjutant general's headquarters. "But I warn you he's a hard man to deal with, and will stick you for a high price."

A few minutes later the rancher accosted the Ranger commander: "I came to buy some fish hooks, and you needn't be stingy with your prices."

"What do you mean," the adjutant general roared.

"Don't get in an uproar," the rancher said. "I'm prepared to pay your own high price."

From the rage of the little dark-haired commander, it was obvious that he was no Jew peddler. "Who sent you here?" he thundered.

The cattleman, equal to the occasion, said: "A fellow down the road."

Jones, a strict disciplinarian, ordered a formal roll-call. He asked the rancher to look the men over and tell him which one sent him.

A true Western sport of the old school, the rancher took a long look, and said: "He ain't here. It was a fellow down the road on horseback."

Jones threatened to disband the company if necessary to find the jokester if such a thing ever happened again.

When the company was dismissed, Jeff slipped off to thank the rancher in private. "I gave him pretty near all the hooks I had," Jeff related.[7]

When times became dull on the frontier, there was no limit to what a man would do to liven things up. The *Colorado Clipper* of April 11, 1885, announced that W. W. Schermerhorn, an attorney of San Angelo, "While under the influence of liquor last week in the saloon of Memph Elliot had his feet badly burned by some unprincipled party pouring alcohol in his boots and setting fire to them." The news item stated that amputation of the lawyer's leg would probably be necessary in order to save his life, and that suit against the saloon proprietor for the amount of $4,000 had been entered.[8]

Gags of the youngsters were not the Little-Lord-Fauntleroy type. Shine Philips tells of a popular get off of his day: Youngsters would load a muzzle-loading shotgun with slugs and sticks and get some uninitiated boy to crawl up on the dam of a waterhole and shoot at somebody's tame ducks. The writer pointed out that the boy shooting the gun got hurt a lot worse than the ducks. More fun still: A "dumb kid" might be convinced of the advantage of putting his shoulder against a post while firing the muzzle-loader. No fatalities were reported, nor were there reports of any repeat performances.[9]

Sometimes the outlander had the last word, though not often. One newcomer made a prophecy about the weather —and after being told that only two kinds of people prophesied on Texas weather—newcomers and damn fools —he had to set up the drinks. He was subjected to considerable "hurrahing," but he bought the drinks and drank his liquor quietly. When the laughing had died down, he leaned calmly against the bar and said slowly: "You say there are only two kinds of people who prophesy about

Texas weather—newcomers and damn fools. You are right. There are only two kinds in Texas." [10]

Some of the sharpest tricks were pulled at the race tracks. During the early years of settlement, the managers of a racecourse, on the Monongahela, near Brownsville, announced a race of one mile heats, purse of $100, for anything "with four legs and hair."

In the settlement there lived a man named Hays, whose custom it was to ride a bull to mill, carrying sacks of corn. Hays determined to enter his bull in the race. So, on several moonlight nights, he took his bull to the grounds, without anyone seeing him, and rode him around the track a few times to show him the lay of the land and to practice him in keeping the right course.

On the day of the race Hays rode his bull onto the grounds. Instead of a saddle, he used a dried oxhide, the head, with horns still on, jogged atop the bull's rump. Hays rode with spurs, and carried a tin horn in his hand.

When he appeared at the judges' stand to enter his bull, the horse owners objected. Hays cited the terms of the announcement, pointed out that his bull had "four legs and hair," and insisted that he had a right to enter him. The argument soon reached the "cussin" stage. The horsemen didn't feel that he was hazarding their chances at the prize money; but "what a dang'd nuisance having a bull, of all things, running around on a race track!"

Hays stood firm, and the judges ruled that according to the announcements, the bull had the right to run.

The horsemen lined up their mounts at the starting post along with the bull, considering the whole thing a gag that would be over as soon as the race started.

W. EGGENHOFER

The starting signal sounded, and the animals took off. Hays blew a blast on his tin horn, and sank his spurs into the bull's sides. The bull bounded forward with a terrifying bellow and at no trifling speed; the dried oxhide flapped up and down, rattling at every bound. Altogether, there was a frightful combination of noises, never heard before on a racecourse. The horses tore out in every direction except down the track, and not one of them could be brought under control in time to beat the bull to the finish line.

The horse owners, red-faced with rage, cried, "Swindle," and contended that Hays was not entitled to the purse; but the spectators, ever on the side of the underdog and enjoying one of the greatest shows ever seen at a race track, were all on the side of the bull. Hays was given the purse.

Then the owners of the horses contended that had it not

★

been for Hays' horn and the oxhide, which should not have been permitted on the ground in the first place, he would not have won.

To the surprise of everyone, Hays told them that his bull could beat them anyway. If they would put up another $100 against the purse he had just won, he would run again without his horn and oxhide.

The racers regarded this as a fool's bet; but anybody who would ride a bull about the community for a saddle horse they considered a little "touched in the head." Furthermore, a man who would enter a bull on a track against race horses was entitled to a good cleaning. To a man, they called his bet.

So the racers lined up for the second heat. At the starting signal, Hays ripped his rowels across the bull's ribs and the animal let out a bellow that all but jumped the horses through their girths. They were nervous already from the first race, and doubtless expected a repeat performance. No pulling on the bits would line the horses down the track with the bull. From that first roaring bellow, the way was all his.

Nobody would have believed that a man could win one race—to say nothing of two—in one day, riding a bull against the fastest horses along the Rio Grande; but Hays did, and from that day on he was known as "Sham." [11]

★

CHAPTER SEVEN

Tough, and Bragging about It

MEN

The Western populace prided itself upon its toughness, and Texans, as a part of it, were never admittedly outdone at anything—certainly not at toughness, or telling about it. They liked to boast that they were equal to any emergency with a sizable margin to spare.

Masculine vigor found expression in such outbursts as:

> Raised in a canebrake,
> Fed in a hog trough,
> Suckled by a she bear,
> The click of a six-shooter is music to my ear.

★

I'm wild and woolly and full of fleas;
I've never been curried below the knees.
I'm a wolf with a barbed-wire tail;
I'm a wolf and it's my night to howl.[1]

Such outbursts as the following were common in the
wild and woolly days: "I'm kin to rattlesnakes on my
mother's side; I'm king of all the eagles an' full brother
to the b'ars! I've put a crimp in a catamount with nothin'
but my living hands! I broke a full-grown alligator across
my knee, tore him asunder an' showered his shrinkin' fragments over a full section of land! I hugged a cinnamon
b'ar to death, an' made a grizzly plead for mercy! Who'll
come gouge with me? Who'll come bite with me?" [2]

Or: "I'm the toughest, wildest killer in the West. When
I'm hungry I bites off the noses of living grizzly b'ars. I
live in a box canyon, where everybody is wild, and shoots
so much they fills the air plumb full of lead, so there ain't
no air to breathe. The further up the canyon you goes, the
wilder the people gets, and I live at the very top end." [3]

A "regular snorter" was described as "half horse, half
alligator, and a bit of snapping turtle. . . ."

A "tough" was expected to recommend himself in his
own way. What he may have lacked in actual strength and
courage, he made up in imagination and rhetoric. "I'm a
waterdog—I'm a snapping turtle. I can lick five times my
own weight in wildcats. I can use up Injens by the cord. I
can swallow niggers whole, raw or cooked. I can out-run,
out-dance, out-jump, out-dive, out-drink, out-holler, and
out-lick any white thing in the shape of human. . . ." [4]

A Texas freighter declared that he had "crossed the

108

ocean on a saw-log; had three sets of teeth and gums for another set; had a double backbone. . . ." [5]

One Texan "would fight a rattlesnake with his bare hands and give the snake three bites to start with." [6] A panhandler, just to show how tough he was, deliberately shot off his wooden foot. [7]

David Crockett became a legend for toughness before he arrived in Texas. Some natives contended that Davy came here because it was the only place left on the frontier tough enough for him. A few statements of prowess attributed to him: "I can run faster, dive deeper, stay under longer, and come out dryer, than any chap this side of the big Swamp. I can outlook a panther and outstare a flash of lightning, tote a steamboat on my back and play rough-and-tumble with a lion." [8]

Cowboys had their own special brand of fire-eating: With two drinks of redeye one puncher offered to go into a bear-biting contest and to ". . . give that thar bear a handicap, he can have first bite."

At the end of the long drives, cowboys like to proclaim their vigor in such fashion as: "I'm too wild to be curried, too tough to be tamed!" [9] And some marshals learned to their sorrow that they were telling the truth.

In the saloons at the trading and shipping centers, cowboys would sing:

> Lions on the mountains; I've drove them to their
> lairs;
> Wild cats are my playmates, and I've wrestled
> grizzly bears;
> Centipedes can't mar my tough old hide;

★

Rattlesnakes have bit me and crawled right off
   and died.

I'm as wild as the horse that roams the range;
Moss grows on my teeth and wild blood's in my
   veins;
I'm wild and woolly and full of fleas, never been
   curried below the knees;
I'm a wild wolf, and this is my night to howl.[10]

There was no end of verses composed by cowboys to
proclaim their rugged background:

Raised in a canebrake, and suckled by a lion,
Head like a bombshell and teeth made out of iron,
Nine rows of jaw teeth and holes punched for more.
I come from ourang-a-tang where the bullfrogs jump
   from north to south.[11]

The braggart needed to know, of course, where and
when it was safe and proper to brag. One tough, in his
exuberance, announced in a crowded saloon that he could
"lick airy fellow that lives in this town." The crowd remained silent. After a few moments, he said in a louder
tone: I can "whip airy man that lives in this county." Still
there was silence. Then he yelled: "I can lick airy man
that lives in West Texas."

At this point, a cowboy rose from a table and said: "I'm
from West Texas, and you can't whip me." With a few
wallops he laid the braggart out flat on the floor.

The victim wobbled to his feet, rubbed his head and exclaimed: "I just took in too much territory." [12]

The boasts of the Bad Man have become a part of the ballads of Texas. The opening stanza of "The Bad Man from the Brazos" is typical:

> I'm a blizzard from the Brazos on a tear,
> > hear me hoot;
> I'm a lifter of the flowing locks of hair,
> > hear me toot;
> I'm a rocker from the Rockies
> And of all the town the talk is,
> "He's a pirate from the Pampas on the shoot."

WOMEN

Men had no monopoly on hardiness. Frontier women, according to the legend, were not the shrinking-violet type that swooned at the sight of a mouse or even a painted Indian. Women were just as much equal to the occasion as men were during the turbulent wilderness days, and the men were proud of it. When they told whoppers about their own extraordinary feats, they included their helpmates.

David Crockett was one of the outstanding promoters of the legend of these rugged, pioneer belles. In his *Almanac* stories, he made his wife the "heroine" of many fanciful tales of backwoods society:

David wrote in his *Almanac* that when he first went courting the future Mrs. Crockett, she had already made a bearskin petticoat, and had one "died red with tiger's

★

blood." On one occasion when she dressed to receive Zebulon Kitchen, a friend of David's, she "combed out her new bearskin petticoat and put on her crocodile skin shortgown, shoes made of buffalo hide, and smoothed down her hair with bear's grease." She looked so attractive, she made David a trifle jealous. She could tell a bear from a panther in the dark by the "feel of his bite." To celebrate on one occasion "she took a bottle of blue lightnin', flogged a she buffalo and milked her, and then walked up to the eagles' nest to get eggs to make her nog." She used scalps to make a patchwork quilt.[13]

One Texas lass, just to keep in trim, used to walk five miles every morning on a barbed-wire fence with a wildcat under each arm.

Another lass "could scalp an Indian, laugh the bark off a pine tree, swim stark [naked] up a cataract, gouge out an alligator's eye, dance a rock to pieces, sink a steamboat, blow out the moonlight, ride a panther bareback, sing a wolf to sleep, and scratch his hide off."

One woman had such an extraordinary mouth that she "could eat victuals with one corner, whistle with the other, and scream in the middle; she could grin with the upper lip and frown all sorts of temptations with the under one; she could scratch the skin of an alligator with her toenail, and snap a ten-foot sarpint's head off by a single galvanic jerk of the tail." [14]

A traveler told of stopping at a frontier home where a woman and her daughter were making soap by boiling the ingredients in a washpot over an open fire in the yard.

The mother shouted: "Watch out there, Mandy! You're standing on a coal of fire."

Mandy looked up and without moving drawled: "Which foot, Ma?" [15]

A practical woman on the frontier was one who did not have to be rescued from bears, panthers, and Indians.

If the women of the backwoods did not have the means or leisure to dress up and shine in parlor society, the menfolk took opportunity to brag about what they were adept at. If they overdid it a little, that was in keeping with the styles of the times.

"DEAD EYES"

Next to hardiness of muscle and constitution, the frontiersmen took pride in their ready marksmanship. According to the old-timers, the Texas gunmen were the most accurate and the quickest on the draw of any trigger artists who ever exploded gunpowder.

Billy the Kid reportedly shot off the heads of six snowbirds as they darted past.[16]

The greatest test of skill seemingly was what a person could do while riding a horse at full speed. Belle Starr, it was said, could gallop at full speed on her horse and knock a bumblebee off a thistle at 50 paces.[17]

Bill Doolin told of the ability of his scout, "Little Bill," to ride at a lope with a six-shooter in each hand and shoot at fence posts on both sides of the road, the shots coming faster than a man could count the reports. Out of ten shots, from five to eight bullets would hit their mark.[18]

Henry Starr supposedly outdid this feat by galloping down the lanes cutting the barbed wire on fences with 45 bullets.[19]

One can hear almost any kind of story about Wild Bill

Hickok shooting at knotholes and "O's" in saloon signs. It appears that he had a passion for fanning a string of shots out of his gun and making a perfect circle around a knothole. To entertain tourists or celebrities, he would shoot inside the double "O's" of saloon signs, the distance depending upon the importance of his particular admirer at the time.[20]

"Eyewitnesses" have testified that they saw Wild Bill at 30 paces draw a six-shooter, and without sighting, drive the cork into a bottle, the bullet going through the bottom of the bottle without smashing it; throw a dime into the air and pierce it with a bullet; hit fence and telegraph wires at every shot while riding full speed.[21]

It is a matter of record that Billy Dixon, during the

Battle of Adobe Walls in 1874, with a buffalo gun, killed
an Indian on horseback three-quarters of a mile away. This
might have been considered an accident with anyone else.
Wyatt Earp, who should have known, said that Dixon was
one of the two best rifle shots then living.[22]

Competition was so keen for shooting honors, a man not
only had to be accurate, he had to be ingenious in devising
stunts. A San Angelo, Texas, outlaw made a reputation by
shooting barrels; but not by any method so prosaic as taking potshots at close range. He would roll the barrel down
a hill and fire six shots from his pistol. There would be six
hits, but only six holes in the barrel. Sounds impossible! It
was nothin' a-tall for the Texas gunman. The outlaw
simply shot through the bung hole each time the barrel
rolled over.[23]

A man took refuge behind a post from Marshal Ben
Thompson in Austin, and attempted to take a shot at Ben.
All Ben could see was a little of his face and one ear sticking out beyond the post. That was enough for Ben; he
called out that he was going to mark him. He did, sending
a bullet neatly through the man's ear.[24]

One of the most talked-of shots in Texas was in San
Antonio—Ben Thompson's shooting of Jack Harris
through the heart when Ben could not even see him. He
knew that Harris was behind a door. Ben fired the fatal
bullet onto a wall; it ricocheted into his target. This
doubtless would have been regarded entirely as a fluke if
anyone else had been shooting; but this was not the first
man Thompson had killed at a time he could not see his
opponent. In Austin, a bartender took a shot at Ben and
ducked behind the bar. Ben quickly calculated the position

115

★

of his attacker and sent a bullet through the wood panel squarely into the bartender's head.[25]

Some marksmanship accounts were reserved. Officers of the law were perhaps better marksmen than the outlaws; but they made less display of their gun work and spoke less of it. Fred Sutton, in *Hands Up*, told of the trial of his friend, Ranger Pat Dooling, in a Panhandle town. Dooling thought there was a plot against him over killing a supposed outlaw, and he refused to admit that he had shot the man. Finally, the judge examined him:

"Did you kill this man?" the judge asked.

"I don't know, sir."

"What? You don't know whether you killed him?"

"No, sir, I do not."

"Did you shoot at him?"

"Yes, sir."

"Did you hit him?"

"I don't know, sir."

After the judge assured the defendant of fair treatment, he again asked him if he had hit the man.

Dooling replied: "Well, sir, if there was one bullet hole in his left nipple and another about an inch below it, both made with a 45, I expect I hit him."

That is exactly where the man was hit—from a distance of 100 feet.[26]

Fred E. Sutton reported seeing Pat Garret, at a range of 40 feet, shoot offhand from the hip at a mark the size of a silver dollar. One bullet cut the bull's eye, one hit an inch below it, another hit an inch above it, and the other two hit six inches from the center. Sutton pointed out that, aimed at the watch charm on a man's front, any of these bullets would have killed him.[27]

The outlaws seem to have had more glamorous publicity than the officers. Al Jennings perfected a highly popular stunt—bouncing an empty tin can along the road ahead of him with bullets from his six-shooters. It is said he could keep the can rolling, without missing a shot, while emptying pistols in both hands.[28]

Another feat that made marksmanship literature concerned a certain badman who, at a distance of 25 yards, cut a string suspending a bottle and then with a second bullet hit the bottle before it struck the ground. The account does not say how much powder he exploded before he made a successful double hit.[29]

The Western gunmen were superb marksmen; but unquestionably their skill has been much improved in the telling. Marksmen, like fortunetellers, make their reputations with their hits. The misses are not remarkable enough to tell about, and are quickly forgotten.

CHAPTER EIGHT

Ingenuity

WORKERS IN RAWHIDE

Ingenuity, which springs in part from individualism, is a Texas legend. The story of Creation is sometimes told in Texas in this fashion: The Lord made the earth in six days, but if He had had some rawhide He could have made it in five.

Texans were never more ingenious than when fashioning rawhide for practical uses. It literally held their world together.

Many babies took their first ride in a rawhide cradle, called a "cooney," a device made by fastening a cow's hide by its four corners under a wagon bed. The cradle served a multitude of other purposes, as a carryall for odds and ends—tools, pots and pans, equipment. The trail drivers used it primarily to carry fuel across the prairies. If the wagon broke down, the drivers trimmed bandages from the cradle to soak and wrap around a broken hub, spoke, or tongue. As the strip of hide dried, the edges of the break drew together with a fastness such as only rawhide could effect.[1]

After living on rawhide, a few Texans lived in and under it. Pants were sometimes made of it, especially in the form of chaps. Even hats were made of it. To fashion these headpieces, a hole about the size of the wearer's head was dug in the ground, and then the wet hide was rammed and stretched into the hole until it became "head-shaped." In the home, this material served scores of needs. Buckets, stools, chairs, were made from it, at least in part. It also served as blankets, or even beds.

Pioneers did most of their household mending with rawhide; they used it as a substitute for nails, often fastening the upright poles around corrals with strips of rawhide. They hung their doors and windows on rawhide hinges. Windows of homes were protected with a kind of clarified rawhide that admitted light. This was a far cry from glass, but on a wild frontier where arrows might be shot into any opening, this was a great comfort,[2] and "it admitted light better than anyone would imagine."

Outside, at his business, the frontier Texan often shod his horse with rawhide, rode a saddle made of it, lassoed his cattle with a riata made of it, even measured his land with a plaited cowhide rope; and, of course, he made most of his whips of cowhide.

Finally, the pioneer might be buried in a rawhide coffin. The French missionary, Domenech, stated that during the terrible cholera epidemic in San Antonio in the late 1840's rawhides served for "biers as well as winding sheets and shrouds. . . Coffins were scarce and corpses were strapped to dried ox-hides and thus dragged along . . . to their graves."

From the cradle to the grave, rawhide was about the handiest item the frontier Texans possessed.

★

George Knight, a cattleman, riding across the Plains was caught in a hailstorm where the stones were "big enough to kill a man." No tree nor any shelter was in sight. He said that he guessed if the stones had not beat some sense into him quick he would have been killed. He saved himself by unsaddling his horse and putting the saddle over his head.[3]

During carpetbag days, a man named Slaughter was arrested in connection with the murder of a Yankee and placed in the stockade at Jefferson. He escaped and started running toward the bayou with the guards in hot pursuit. Slaughter was a one-armed man and consequently a handicapped swimmer. At the bank of the bayou, he tossed a rock into the water at the opposite side and quickly hid. The guards, hearing the noise and seeing the water disturbed on the opposite side of the stream, immediately crossed over and began a hunt there. Slaughter, with his pursuers across the bayou from him, quietly slipped away to safety.[4]

One day in Kerrville a horse fell into a cistern 30 feet deep. This caused distress among the population . . . that is, until someone explained that the solution was as simple as pouring water—into a cistern; and so the cistern was filled with water and the horse floated out.[5]

There was a time when most butter was made at home. And if there is a house job that is nearly universally hated by menfolk, it's churning. M. Ramsey, a farmer living near Mt. Pleasant, discovered a way to churn and do a man's work at the same time. He placed a jar containing clabbered milk in a sack and tied the sack to his saddle.[6]

When he came in from his riding chore, the butter was made.

JACK RABBITS SHOT WITH GOLD BULLETS

Colonel Roberts, one-time Texan Ranger, "molded" possibly the most ingenious bullets ever used to shoot jack rabbits—slugs of pure gold.

In the summer of 1835, Colonel Roberts, with several other traders, made an 800-mile trading trip from Independence, Missouri, to Santa Fé, where they sold their goods for a handsome profit. With the proceeds of their sales in gold and silver coin, they started on the return trip.

About 300 miles out, Indians stampeded their horses one night and took off after them. Thus the traders were left stranded with their treasure-laden wagons 500 miles from home and over 200 miles from the nearest settlement. It was too late in the season for west-bound traders, and they knew that no caravans were following them. No help could be expected from any source. There was only one chance of survival—escape from the wagons before the Indians returned after capturing the horses.

The men decided to turn back toward the Rio Grande. They took their guns and ammunition for protection, and to procure food on the long journey. A few of the men could not resist the temptation to pocket a few of the shining doubloons they had risked so much to earn.

For days, the men trudged across the hot desert. Provisions soon gave out, and they had to depend upon what game they could kill. Jack rabbits were about all they found. They did not complain about the quality of the food, but the animals were so small they made a heavy

★

drain upon the ammunition. Days before the journey ended, every shot had been used.

The gold and silver coins the men carried, though once the most valuable possession, appeared now the most worthless. Then, someone had a truly "golden" idea: Gold actually might save them, though they could buy nothing with it. The men took their butcher knives and chopped the yellow doubloons into bullets. Then, with the golden slugs, they shot jack rabbits for food. These bullets furnished the margin of food that saved their lives.

Colonel Roberts made his way into Texas and joined the Rangers to make another stake.[7]

INDIVIDUALISTS IN FACE OF DEATH

Perhaps the most radical individual in regard to death was Brit Bailey. He was in Texas before Austin showed up, and held a squatter's claim on a piece of land included in Austin's grant. Austin told him he would have to get off, but nobody ever had much luck telling Brit Bailey what to do. He lived his life out on his claim.

In his last sickness, when he knew the end was near, he said to his wife: "I have never looked up to any man, and when I'm in my grave I don't want it said, 'There *lies* Brit Bailey.' Bury me standing up with my face to the setting sun. I have been all my life traveling westward and I want to face that way when I die."

So his widow, in compliance with his strange request, had a grave dug like a well; and the rugged old pioneer was lowered into the Western earth he had loved and fought for, feet first, facing the setting sun.

In 1867 when the great yellow-fever epidemic broke out

in Houston, the city was in the process of being "reconstructed" by Yankee soldiers. One of the most uncompromising Rebels in all the South was "Old Man" Pannel, Houston's only undertaker. Because of his bitter hatred for and bitter language directed at the Yankees, he had several times been brought before the commander under guard.

During the epidemic, it became impossible for Pannel to bury the dead fast enough. An alarming number of dead soldiers began to accumulate. Again the undertaker was arrested and brought before the commanding officer, who said: "Mr. Pannel, they tell me you dislike to bury my soldiers."

"General," Pannel snorted, "whoever told you that told you a damn lie. It's the pleasantest thing I've had to do in years and I can't get enough of it. I would like to bury every damn one of you."

The general ordered Pannel to jail; but he was soon released because his services were in such demand. Pannel had his revenge. "You see," he later said, "these Yankees think a nigger is as good as they are and better than we are, so I'm giving them their own medicine. I'm mixing up the cards, so to speak. I plant a nigger and then I plant a white soldier. Sometimes I put a white one with three or four niggers and then I reverse it and put a nigger with three or four white ones. Those relatives up North are going to have a time getting things straightened out. Chances are some nigger is going to rest under a big tombstone meant for a white man." [8]

Grim necessity often forced frontier "undertakers" to resort to crude but practical means at hand. The wife of a man who had died in Texas wrote from the East begging

123

★

that her husband's body be sent home. The body was cured like a piece of pork, smoked, packed in two barrels joined end to end, and shipped by boat.[9]

The bodies of 17 Texans who were doomed to death by the "black bean" drawing at Mier, Mexico, in 1843, were brought back for burial in Texas soil; but it wasn't easy five years later. Their comrades collected their bones in 17 tow sacks and carried them 300 miles for burial on Monument Bluff near La Grange.[10]

OUTWITTING THE INDIANS

Frontier Texans were notably ingenious at escaping from hostile Indians. In this art, grim necessity was the mother of many life-saving inventions.

A salty old scout and hunter called "Uncle Seth," while skinning a deer one day about four miles from a surveyor's camp, was jumped by a band of Indians. He leaped onto his horse, which was a good sprinter; but after about a mile the Indians started gaining on him. As he said, he had to outsmart them on what they thought they knew about white men. He raced to a thicket, jumped off his horse, tied him to a bush at the edge, ran through the thicket and on to camp on foot. The Indians, always cautious about crowding a man they could not see, doubtless assumed that their intended victim was hiding there with a bead drawn on the nearest Indian. Uncle Seth returned for his horse with a party. Moccasin tracks were thick around the thicket, but none within 50 yards of the horse.[11]

Big Foot Wallace told of a writer, uninitiated in the ways of the frontier, traveling with his party, who, at the last moment, saved his life by his wits. He "whipped" a

124

whole band of Indians with a "weapon" he had been carrying which had made him the joke of the party—an umbrella. Just as his horse was winded, and the savages were literally breathing down his neck, he wheeled his horse, pulled his umbrella from behind his saddle and flipped it open right in the eyes of the Indians' horses. They stopped as if frozen for a second. Then they wheeled and stampeded in the direction whence they came; and nothing the Indians could do would turn them—if, indeed, the Indians actually wanted to turn them. The tenderfoot rode into camp at his leisure.[12]

W. P. Brashear saved his scalp by quick thinking one morning in 1839. While examining a tract of land in Lavaca County, about ten miles from the Henseley settlement, he suddenly discovered about 20 Comanches racing toward him on their mustang ponies. Brashear put spurs to his horse, heading him toward the settlement. He was unarmed, but he had no great fear because he considered his mount one of the fastest in the country, able to outdistance any mustang pony.

Before Brashear had traveled a mile, however, he was alarmed to see the Indians gaining on him. It was obvious that, if something were not done quickly, the Indians would soon overhaul him.

In front of him, about a mile away, was a creek aptly called "Boggy," which could be forded only in a few places. In this desperate moment, an idea for a stratagem struck Brashear. If he could just stay out of arrow range for another mile he might save himself. He applied whip and spurs to his horse, demanding his best for a spurt.

He was able momentarily to outdistance the Comanches.

He reached the creek about 600 yards below a ford. Brashear took advantage of the cover of a fringe of timber bordering the creek to dash up the stream unobserved by the Indians. He crossed the creek, and then raced down the other side to the approximate location where he had entered the timber on the opposite side. The Indians approached the point where Brashear had entered the woods just in time to see him galloping off directly before them.

The Indians did just what Brashear thought they would do—they concluded, with reasonable logic, that he had crossed the stream at that point. Without delay, they plunged into the stream to be piled up on a jumble of horses sinking to their necks in quicksand.

Brashear was able to ride safely into the settlement.[13]

Sixty-odd years had not dimmed the mind of William Barton. One afternoon, in 1842, with his gun across his shoulder, he walked over the hill to the north of his home

for a view of the prairie. As he passed a thicket, a group of
Indians sprang up and shot at him, one bullet grazing the
brim of his hat. Barton leveled his Kentucky rifle and
fired, wounding one of his attackers.

It was soon evident, however, that there were too many
Indians to stand off in a pitched battle. So Barton wheeled
and took to his heels in the direction of his home. The Indians immediately set out after him. Before Barton reached
the crest of the hill, his years began to tell. His strength
began failing rapidly. He realized that he would never be
able to outrun the savages to safety.

In this emergency, he thought of his deer dogs. He
called for them to come to his assistance, and a half-dozen
hounds came bounding toward him.

Then, just as relief seemed at hand, there occurred about
as unlucky a break as any man could ever expect: When
the dogs were almost to him, a deer crossed their path and
they took off after it. For the second time, in a matter of
seconds, the old gentleman's scalp was as good as hanging
on an Indian's belt. Again only his wits could save him.

Seldom has a man had two good life-saving tricks in the
bag to fit one emergency; but William Barton did that
afternoon. He had an idea—if he could just make it to the
top of the hill. The Indians were rapidly gaining on him,
but confidence in his plan gave him renewed hope and
strength, and, with almost superhuman strength for a man
his age, he sprinted ahead and held his distance for the
seconds necessary to reach the brow of the hill.

Now that he could see over the hill, and the Indians
could not, he stopped suddenly, and called in a loud voice:
"Here they are, boys; come quick!" In the meantime, he

★

beckoned with one hand to the boys who were not there, and with the other he pointed toward the Indians.

The Indians, supposing that a party of Texans was over the hill rushing to the aid of their intended victim, did not wait to meet the imaginary enemy but fled in the opposite direction.[14]

Davy Crockett saved himself from the Comanches by playing up two attributes most impressive to the Indians—courage and physical strength. According to his account, about 100 Comanches rode up on Crockett. Their numbers, and the suddenness of their approach made flight or resistance futile.

It so happened that in a hand-to-paw combat, Crockett had just killed a huge lion, the carcass of which was present. This attracted the Indians' attention and before they had time to decide upon his fate he started telling the story of his victorious struggle with the ferocious beast. Several of the Indians understood English and were entranced by the account of the fight. Crockett told how a rifle ball had only maddened the animal, causing it to spring upon him. They had grappled in deadly combat, had tumbled down a high bluff together, and finally he had stabbed the cougar to death with his hunting knife. To further illustrate his story, Crockett displayed fresh scars on his body from teeth and claws.

The Indians obviously decided such a brave fighter should not be put to death. He was spared for a more glorious death—at the Alamo.[15]

There is at least one case on record where "unnecessary talk" by the fair sex proved necessary. This prolonged "small talk" probably saved their lives.

128

In February of 1839, a party of Indians attacked the Coleman home near the Colorado, killed Mrs. Coleman and a son, named Albert, and took another son prisoner.

Two little sisters were left alone in the house when their brother Albert, a lad of 15, died defending the home. The little girls had taken protective cover under a bed; and now they did all that was left to them, that they knew to do, to save their lives. They talked, carrying on a continuous conversation with each other, as they had been told to do. It was supposedly the sound of voices in the house that dissuaded the Indians from entering. Thus, the little girls "talked" themselves out of a very close place.[16]

Possibly no soldier ever faced the fire of battle with more calm courage than Mrs. John Baggett. On the late afternoon of March 3, 1857, ten whooping, painted Comanche warriors swooped down upon the Baggett ranch near the North Leon River, where Mrs. Baggett was alone with nine children. She did not even have a gun, and there was no chance to run away.

The mother was able to get seven of the children into the house while the Indians were catching the horses; but two of the children, Joel, 12, and Betty, ten, were playing under a live-oak tree some distance from the cabin and were intercepted.

The savages stripped all the clothes from the children. Then they proceeded slowly to torture Joel by lancing him with arrows. Obviously, the Indians thought this mutilation and the shrieks of the child would bring the mother out of the cabin and expose her and the other children. When this torture failed to bring the mother, the attacker scalped the little boy alive and hung the trophy on

★

a belt already containing the recognizable red-haired scalp of a neighbor.

Joel died in a short time of his wounds. Then the Indians proceeded to lance Betty. After piercing her body a score or more times, they turned her loose to go staggering and bleeding toward the cabin door. The little girl fainted twice before reaching the house; but finally she approached the door. The mother, mindful of the tactics of the Indians, and still maintaining her mental faculties in the face of the calamity, did not open the door for the child. Instead, she calmly said to the little girl through the cracks: "Betty, go around to the other door; the Indians will kill us all if Mamma opens this door."

The Indians, failing to get the door open, rode off. Mrs. Baggett lost one son; but through self-control and presence of mind, she saved eight other children and herself.[17]

One white captive, allowed to go hunting with his captors, made a practice of getting "lost," and staying lost for progressively longer periods each time until he was able to get a sufficient start on the Indians to remain "lost."

Sometimes, simple means were sufficient to outwit the Indians. On one occasion, a large party of Indians attacked Quihi, in Midland County. As the howling, painted savages swarmed onto the town, it seemed that nothing could save it from destruction; but, at the darkest moment, one of the citizens, Mo Brucks, ran to the church and started ringing an old bell brought over from Germany. This so frightened the Indians that they abandoned their attack and ran off.

The white man, of course, did not always win; but whether it was a scheme that worked or failed, the frontiersman, in the presence of hostile Indians, usually thought of something—pretty fast.

LEGENDARY INDIVIDUALIST

Even the fictitious heroes of Texas are rugged individualists with a definite turn for the extraordinary. They are fairy-book characters with brawn instead of flimsy wings, ingenuity instead of wands, and they are individualists instead of members of a caravan. As individualists, Texas folk heroes are more fabulous than story-book fairies. Fairies had their origin in the days of kings, and those benevolent creatures usually worked in groups and took their orders from central authority.

Not the Texas "hero." He takes orders from nobody. Just turn him loose—don't hamper him—and he'll do almost anything the imagination can conceive. There are no collectivists among Texas folk heroes. There doubtless have been some such characters in the land, but they never rated the literary bandwagon.

Paul Bunyan was an adopted Texan. He couldn't have missed Texas. In the Northwest, he was the tree-choppingest lumberjack that ever slung an ax. Once he hit the Texas oil fields, he was the well-diggingest fool that ever stuck a bit into the Texas earth. He drove spikes to the head with one blow of his eight-pound hammer, and in a single day built derricks so high that the derrick man was able to come down only twice a month for payday.

Texas folk heroes are hardy, independent characters all. Pecos Bill, as an infant, choked a rattlesnake to death with his bare hands and stole its ten rattles. He didn't cry for his pa to call a government exterminator. His pet cow,

★

Patience, had five calves at once, and she wasn't fed on government hay. He operated the Perpetual Motion Ranch—let it alone and it would run itself.

There was Praxiteles Swan, the fighting preacher who defied the bishops of his conference along with the Yankees. He is the personification of the individualist in the church, and is recognized poetically as a composite of the fearless Texas ministers who were not afraid to back their convictions with anything from the Bible to a cannon.[18]

These heroes could not live long and with such popularity without leaving their imprint upon the real Texas population. A complete list of such individualists would be almost endless.

Texas to this day is inclined to leave Europe to its collectivism and its effeminate fairies. They prefer the hardy individualists, like Paul Bunyan, Pecos Bill, and the Reverend Swan.

CHAPTER NINE

Thirsty Texans

FEARLESS DRINKERS

Most of the male population of early Texas drank whisky, and didn't give a hoot who knew it. Before the days of soda pop chasers and bubble water, men drank their whisky straight when they were thirsty, without taking to the bushes or pulling down the shades.

Much blood has been shed in Texas over watering places; but to some hardy frontiersmen, though water was worth fighting for, it was fit only for stock to drink; of course, when families came on, it was mighty handy for women and children.

Some of the world's most expressive compliments to excellence of whisky have originated in Texas. One pioneer, praising his jug of spirits, announced: "It's like the juice of women's tongues and panther hearts, for after drinking it, I can talk forever and fight the devil."

To some thirsty souls, taking a drink took precedence over everything—including retreating to safety before an enemy. During the Revolution, the Rangers at Bastrop became so overconfident that the Mexicans would not attack there, that they had only one sentry out when an army of about 600 of the enemy appeared on the opposite side of the river. There were only 32 Rangers, so a hasty retreat was the only practical maneuver. In the haste of retreat, the sentry, an old man by the name of Jimmie Curtis, was left behind at his post. As the Rangers rode away, one of them, Noah Smithwick, galloped back to find the old sentry sitting with his back to a tree, with a bottle of whisky beside him, "as happy and unconscious of danger as a turtle on a log." "Uncle Jimmie, mount and ride for your life," Smithwick called as he drew his horse to a halt. "The Mexicans are on the other side and our men are all gone."

"The hell they are!" replied the old man calmly. "Light and take a drink."

"There's no time for drinking. Come, mount and let's

be off. The Mexicans may swim the river and be after us any minute," the impatient Smithwick warned.

"Then, let's drink to their confusion," Uncle Jimmie insisted.

Smithwick, deciding the quickest way to get the old man moving was to oblige him, dismounted to take a drink with him.

Now anyone versed in the delicacies of this type of imbibing will tell you that it is a thing not to be rushed. Uncle Jimmie was indisputably a connoisseur, and nothing, including an army of 600 Mexicans, would make him display crudeness in this basic social act. So the drinks were taken leisurely with Smithwick keeping one eye on the Mexicans.

When, at length, the men rode off, Uncle Jimmie said: "Well, we can say one thing; we were the last men to leave." [1]

Statutory prohibition did not bring the first court rulings concerning whisky in Texas. Judges generally took what they considered a practical course regarding such matters— at least practical enough to suit the citizenry—which, after all, is the basic duty of a politician. Judge Robert E. B. Baylor was holding district court in Bastrop, when news came that the bill for Texas' annexation had passed the United States Congress and had received the approval of President Polk. In announcing the glad tidings, the judge quoted Chief Justice Marshall as saying, "No man should be considered drunk on Independence Day, so long as he can pronounce the word 'Epson.' " [2] Baylor added that in his opinion the same rule should apply to that occasion, and

★

he promptly adjourned court until ten o'clock the following morning in order that the town might celebrate.

DETERMINED DRINKERS

Even imprisonment did not necessarily alleviate the big thirst. Bishop and Giles tell of a man arrested in Tascosa in December, 1881, who was shackled and placed in Jack Rayan's saloon, there being no jail convenient. The prisoner's arms, however, were left free. During the night, he tore his blanket into strips and fashioned them into a rope. With his improvised lariat, he lassoed whisky bottles from the shelf behind the bar and enjoyed the night well enough.[3]

Back in the times that some people refer to as "the good old days when beer sold for ten cents per bucket," a few imbibers, long on taste and short on funds, discovered a way of stretching a short beer into a long one—a little longer, at least. They greased the inside of the bucket with butter before presenting it to the bartender to be filled. Result: All beer, no foam.

Only determined, hardy men could have thrived on some of the early brands of liquor. Stuart N. Lake wrote: "Raw alcohol colored with coffee was commonly offered in the guise of whisky, the sting heightened by red pepper and the flavor toned with tobacco. The popularity of a whisky-wagon was determined by the mixture dispensed over its tailboard; as customers judged liquor by the 'bite' it took on the way down and the speed of its strangle-hold after swallowing."[4]

Terrible reports—even terrible facts—about specific brands of liquor seemed to advertise rather than stop sales

136

of it. A buffalo-skinner named Thompson turned whisky peddler and built up a tremendous business on the Plains, because of the kick his spirits had. Then one day a thief made off with one of his empty barrels. Inside, the thief found a half-dozen strangely familiar-looking objects. He held a conference with some of the heavy drinkers. Then they accosted Thompson: "These are snake heads, ain't they? Rattlesnake heads?"

Thompson admitted that he always put half a dozen rattlesnake heads in each barrel of whisky. "They give power to the liquor," he announced with professional pride.

He was told to get out of town; but the exposure did him no apparent harm. Rather it advertised him. For years he sold whisky from a barrel over a great portion of the West. He was universally known as Snakehead Thompson.[5]

Frontier ministers campaigned against the demon drink. "Taking the pledge" was a regular ritual at the camp meetings, though there was usually a dispensary in the bushes conveniently near the church arbor. Many repenters "went on the book" in the heat of the summer meetings and were taken off before the cold weather had lasted until Christmas. A typical paragraph from church history: "Elder R. G. Green joined by letter December, 1838, and was excluded for drunkenness in February, 1840." [6]

Mody C. Boatright tells of an apparently "typical" frontiersman who was converted and joined the Methodist Church at the age of 50. He refused to give up liquor, though he never drank to excess. His pastor urged him to quit drinking, saying that although it did not hurt him, it might be a bad influence on others. He held out for years

★

sticking to his point that he could absolutely "pray better on the outside of a pint of whisky." [7]

HEAVY DRINKERS

A frontier Texan, celebrating with his friends one Saturday night, looked up the street and said: "Look, there goes old Bill Jones. The old fool's going home this early; and look at him. He's got a whole sack of flour on his shoulder, and I'll bet he ain't got a drop of whisky in his house!"

This attitude probably represented a sizable segment of frontier opinion on the matter of liquor. By the time of the Revolution, the reputation of the Texans as drinkers had become international—at least it was something of a tradition among the Mexicans. One of the few Mexicans who escaped from San Jacinto explained the slaughterous attack: "The Americans were all drunk." He said the Mexicans had them whipped when a boat loaded with whisky came up. The Americans then "all filled up with corn juice, and yelling, 'Alamo, Alamo,' made a wild rush for the Mexicans, falling upon them with clubs, and beat their brains out."

Often whisky was more readily available than water, particularly on the dry plains. Louis Schorp told of a cattle inspector, who, on finding no water at hand to wet a brand, took out a whisky bottle, "wet the brand with the liquor, smoothed the hair," and the brand showed very plainly.[8] Some people who were not professed drinkers carried the beverage for medicinal purposes. Many thought it was the best treatment ever discovered for snake bite.

Lack of finances may have saved some imbibers from

drinking themselves to death. An Irishman, named Fitzgerald, who owned a small oyster stand in Houston, inherited a considerable amount of property. He immediately kicked his oyster counter over and devoted all his time to drinking. About the time he became a physical wreck, his fortune gave out—a coincident that probably saved his life. When Fitzgerald finally sobered up, and his hands were steady enough to work, he reopened his oyster stand.

About six months later, his lawyer came in again and told him that he had inherited more property—a greater amount than before. "Get out of here," he stormed at the lawyer. "I wouldn't get on another drunk like that for the whole city of Houston."

Much to the disgust of the lawyer, Fitzgerald looked up all the people to whose property he had a claim and gave them a clear title; he knew of only one thing to spend surplus money for—liquor. As he figured it, his system just could not take another fortune's worth of it.

His meager oyster business kept him about as temperate as his constitution demanded. He explained the matter of giving his property away: "No use in letting money kill me!"

N. A. Jennings gave his estimate of the potency of one brand of pioneer firewater: "There are about five fighting drunks in a quart bottle of mescal, and subsequently five splitting headaches." [9]

Probably the Karankawa Indians knew their capacities about as well as anyone, and were about as practical drinkers. At least they had a system. When they went on a "spiritual rampage," they divided their members. Half of

★

the party remained sober while the other half imbibed. Next time, the order was reversed.

THE "HUMOROUS" LEGEND

Nothing—including trouble, lack of women, or psychoneurosis—has ever created such a determination for a drink like telling a Texan he can't have one. About half the population has been concerned with making liquor-drinking inconvenient or embarrassing for the other half. All of which has made the first half feel noble and possessed of a mission and made the other half acutely determined not to have anything put over on them. It has been a highly amusing contest, furnishing material for literary treatment much better than that ordinarily made of it by the Anti-Saloon League or the brewers' friend, Owen P. White, who said that "whisky, which destroyed weaklings, had its own way of building up great men for Texas."

Possibly if the population had not chosen sides in this matter, drinking whisky would never have appeared any funnier than drinking milk; but funny it is today to many observers, much the type of amusement of a fun-house where a gust of wind blows the ladies' skirts up. To be caught drinking by the Antis is a like exposé—a supposed surprise to the imbiber as if a gust of high-pressure air had blown the moral coverings from about him and revealed his thirsty, naughty soul.

The fine points of the humor of drinking I leave to the psychologists and repeat a few samples of drinking "wit":

It is said that Governor O. M. Roberts, during his law-teaching days at the University of Texas, excused himself from class one day to take something for a severe cold. A student, suspecting the professor's remedy, asked: "Governor, don't you think a better remedy could be found for cough and colds than whisky?"

"Young man," exclaimed Roberts, "who would want a better remedy?"

A West Texas cattleman waked up in a hotel room after a celebration of the night before, grabbed the water pitcher and drained it before setting it down. Then he said: "If I'd a-known water tasted so good, I'd a-dug a well a long time ago."

The actress, Lily Langtry, offered a public drinking fountain to the town of Langtry named for her. Judge Roy Bean, the story goes, respectfully declined the gift, because, as he wrote her: "Water is the one thing people *don't* drink around here."

General David Twiggs, noted for his drinking habits, summoned a lieutenant, named Arthur D. Tree, before him on a charge of off-duty drinking in a manner reflecting discreditably upon the Service. The lieutenant's reply to his commanding general was such as to bring only an official caution: "Sir, I can only say to the general that as the twig is bent, so is the tree inclined." [10]

One frontier patriarch long had been the consternation of the Drys by his habit of drinking a gourd full of whisky every morning. On the eve of his 99th birthday, he passed away. A neighbor gave the news to a member of the Anti-Saloon League, who responded: "So whisky finally got him?"

CHAPTER TEN

Games of Chance

BIG TIME

Most of the settlers of Texas were speculators of one sort or another. They risked their fortunes and lives against great odds in an insecure and wild country. Therefore, it is no surprise that in their moments of relaxation, the gambling instinct stayed with them. As long as gambling was a matter of pitting skill against skill, most gamblers were respected on the frontier. Stuart N. Lake stated: "The list of prominent Western citizens, from bank presidents and preachers on down, who in early days were gamblers and saloon keepers, is well-nigh endless. . . . As long as they dealt fairly with their fellows, no one thought less of them for their calling." [1]

Bat Masterson, one of the most noted gamesters of the Old West, won a gold-headed cane on the Fourth of July, 1885, as the "most popular man in Dodge City." [2]

The austere Stephen F. Austin tried to stop gambling in his colony by passing laws against the practice. The laws did little good. During the first year of the Republic, laws were enacted against gambling, but the wild, daring edge had not worn off the reckless frontiersmen; the games continued. An editorial in the *Houston Weekly Times* of April 30, 1840, stated: "Since the law for the suppression of gambling has been passed, we have seen more card playing than ever. New games have been instituted and old ones revived. The Texans play at rounders; the Frenchmen at vingt-et-un; the Mexicans at Monte; the Kentuckians, Mississippians, and Tennesseeans at poker; the Dutch at euchre; the Sons of Erin at forty-five; and the Negroes at old sledge." [3]

Passing laws against gambling served to make games of chance more complicated, and apparently more interesting. William R. Hogan states that the records of the Republic reveal more indictments for gambling than for any other offense. [4]

From the time the first law was passed, sporting men began hunting ways to circumvent the statute. On one occasion a group of Houston lawyers, doctors, and businessmen were indicted for participating in a poker game, an embarrassing situation for citizens of such prominence. They sought out a legal wit by the name of Colonel Manley, who got them released on a rather revealing technicality. He won the case on the grounds that there was a bed in the room in which the game took place, and a bedroom was not a public place in the meaning of the law. From that time on this group felt much safer when playing poker if there was a bed in the room—and there usually was. [5]

Gambling was no mere penny-ante pastime on the frontier. In the 1890's, the leading merchants of Amarillo, according to a report in the *Amarillo News and Globe*, bought playing cards in carload lots, and saloons bought

★

them in case lots.[6] A case contained 480 decks, about one week's supply for the ordinary saloon.

Shanghai Pierce, the noted Texas cattleman, is said to have offered the State of Nebraska $10,000 annually for the exclusive right to deal monte on railway trains within the borders of that state.[7]

A Mississippi planter named John A. Scott won some Texas land scrip in a game in New Orleans. Believing the certificates worthless, he tossed them into an old trunk. A quarter-century later, they were found; and "when the Dallas and Wichita Railroad was proposed in 1876, Scott's heirs duly filed their scrip and located the present city of Wichita Falls."[8] The complete list of such important poker transactions would fill a book.

As late as 1883, a faction of businessmen in Dallas opposed the district attorney's campaign to drive the gamblers out of town. A delegation called upon him to point out how bad such a move would be for business, that it would slow down prosperity, "that Fort Worth with a shrewder policy was offering the gamblers free rents and $35,000 to remove to that city."[9]

THOSE ENDURING GAMES

Once a poker game got started it was harder to stop than a grass fire. Wyatt Earp told of being routed out of bed to provide wood to keep a game going until morning. He was paid $100 per cord and $10 for a helper.[10] To win all the cash a player had was not necessarily sufficient to stop his game. If he was known, he might play to the value limit of his word or note. A young cowman was "gambling his life away" at a monte table, with a rich

144

cattleman backing him, his cattle as security. When he had lost $20,000 the backer told him that was as far as he could go.

"You can't let me have any more?" the reckless youngster pleaded.

"That's all your cattle are worth," the man answered.

The young cattleman pulled his pistol, shot himself through the head, slumped dead onto the table, and then rolled onto the floor. The game went on.[11]

There is at least one instance where an impending hanging did not stop a game. N. A. Jennings tells of a game at Beeville in the cell of Ed Singleton, who was waiting to be hanged the next morning: "That night I passed in Singleton's cell with three other Rangers. . . . All night long, I played 'seven-up' with Singleton. We played for $10 a game—on trust."[12] Once started, the game never stopped until the sheriff broke it up next morning to hang the gambling prisoner.

Proof of crookedness did not necessarily stop a game. There is the classic about two men who got stuck in a lonely town. Finally, one found a game where he could pass the time. After slight observation, his partner urged him to stop.

"The game's crooked!" he declared.

"I know it," the player replied, "but it's the only game in town!"

There is the old one about a poker game in which four men, one of them one-eyed, were playing. Suddenly one man jerked out his pistol and said: "I ain't calling no names, but the next fellow I see dealing from the bottom of the deck I'm gonna shoot his other eye out!"

A poker player yanked his six-shooter out and shouted: "This game ain't honest! Pecos Pete ain't playin' the hand I dealt him."

But the games went on.

LUCK AND SUPERSTITION

Even the scientific gamblers and "system" players never completely discarded the element of luck. Limpie Lewie, one of Houston's most colorful gamblers, described his run of luck: "It was chicken one day and feathers the next." One pioneer Texan said his luck was so good one winter that, if life had been a poker game, he "could have drawn to a cow chip and caught a yoke of oxen." [13]

Almost every gambler, it seems, had his own set of superstitions; and he usually ridiculed those of his colleagues. Dr. S. O. Young relates an incident that occurred in Galveston while riding on a horse-drawn streetcar with a "distinguished journalist" who was a "sport." In the midst of a conversation, he jumped to his feet, grabbed the rope, began jerking it wildly and shouting to the driver to stop.

A funeral procession was observed passing down the intersection street just ahead of the car.

"Why, that fellow liked to have ruined me," the sporting journalist wailed. "He was going to pull us right through that funeral. I had that to happen to me once and I never held a thing for six months." [14]

Dr. Young wrote of another friend who would abandon any business enterprise for the day if he met a cross-eyed woman face to face. He claimed, "Such a meeting is absolutely fatal and every particle of luck abandons me right then and there." [15]

In the early days, gamblers were often handicapped by lack of small change. It became a custom to cut a silver dollar into four pieces to use as quarters. This might have proved a workable system, but gamblers have a tendency to stretch things—other than their luck. They started stretching a silver dollar into five quarters. The dollar was cut into five pieces; with a little extra hammering, each piece could be made to pass as a quarter. Gamblers had so beat up the silver currency by the time Mexico won her independence that the situation influenced the new government to immediately change the stamp of her coin. [16]

INDIAN GAMBLERS

Many white people took advantage of the Indians' instinct to gamble; but the white man did not always find the Indians an easy prize. The story of an Indian buck

★

named Mulaquetop and the horse race he pulled off at old Fort Chadbourne will illustrate the Indians' craftiness:

Mulaquetop was a subchief of the Comanches. When he and his band camped near the fort, the soldiers regarded them as nuisances. However, they knew that Mulaquetop was something of a sport.

Many of the officers owned some of the best horses in the land and took great pride in racing them. So, in order to have a little fun and excitement, in this isolated post, the officers bantered Mulaquetop for a race. The Indian showed slight interest; but he hung around, giving the horse owners opportunity to insist. After several days maneuvering, he let the officers talk him into running against the third best horse at the fort.

Mulaquetop showed up at the course with such a miserable looking pony that some of the officers decided they should not have matched their third best horse. They would not get their bets called. Any horse that had not been pulling a wagon all day should outrun this pitiful creature, they reasoned. The pony had legs like "gate posts," and a three-inch coat of rough hair that stuck out from ears to tail and showed no evidence of ever having been touched by shears or brush.

The jockey, a stalwart buck of 170 pounds, looked big enough to carry the animal on his shoulders.

To the surprise of the soldiers, however, the Indians bet their robes and other possessions against money and provisions.

The jockey approached the starting line armed with a huge club. At the signal, he started belaboring the poor beast and did not let up until the finish. To the astonishment of the soldiers, the Indian pony won by a neck.

The whites proposed another race. This time the second best garrison horse would run. Again Mulaquetop was not eager; but after much dickering he accepted. The bets were doubled. In less than an hour the race started, with the same jockey with the same club on the same "sheep" of a pony.

The second race was a duplicate of the first. The shaggy pony won by a neck.

The officers, disgusted, and hurt in pride, proposed a third race against their prize racer, a thoroughbred Kentucky mare, known to beat all challengers at least 40 yards in 400. The Indians accepted, and piled up everything they could raise.

This time, at the start, the Indian rider threw away his club and let out a great war whoop at which the horse pricked up his ears and left his competition several lengths behind. Making hideous faces at his opposing rider and beckoning to him to come on, Mulaquetop rode the last 50 yards of the race sitting with his face to the pony's tail.

Cleaning the soldiers at Fort Chadbourne was a small-time operation for Mulaquetop. Actually, his shaggy horse was on vacation, having just cleaned out the Kickapoos to the tune of 600 ponies.[17]

★

Apothecaries and Healers

REGULATED MEDICINE

One of the constant problems faced by the early Texans was that of preserving health. Without hospitals, scientific equipment, or adequate doctors, the pioneers used many queer remedies in an attempt to keep body and soul together.

Spanish Texas did not have socialized medicine, but the government took a strong hand in matters of public health and medical treatment. Doctors had little freedom in choosing or rejecting patients or in determining the manner of treating them. Possibly the first royal order regulating medical practice in Texas was issued in 1777—to the effect that surgeons, before notifying the authorities, were to attend any person wounded by violence or accident who might summon them or call at their home. Afterward, they were required to notify the Royal Judge without loss of time. Practitioners were subject to heavy penalties for any infraction of the law. For a first offense, the surgeon was subject to a fine of 25 pesos; second offense called for a fine of 50 pesos and two years exile 20 leagues

150

from the practitioner's residence; the third offense called for a fine of 100 pesos and four years in prison.[1]

A strict and precise royal cedula was issued in 1804 concerning Caesarean operations: ". . . The person who is waiting on a pregnant patient shall notify the priest of the parish as soon as she dies. If the priest happens to be a surgeon, he shall after being certain of the actual death of the pregnant patient arrange for the Caesarean operation by means of and according to the rules of the aforesaid instructions which he ought to have before him for its exact performance. If the priest is not a surgeon, the operation will be performed by the surgeon of the town. . . . The priest as well as the physician who may be called for this purpose should go at any hour, night or day, to the house of the deceased. . . . In towns where there is no physician, the parish priest shall agree with the judicial authority in the selection of the man they consider most capable and best prepared to perform the Caesarean operation. . . . He (the priest) must not consent to the burial of anyone, regardless of class, who may have died in childbirth, unless he knows that the operation has been performed." Any deviation from royal instructions in this matter brought serious penalties.[2]

On April 13, 1804, the king issued a royal order giving instruction for "the safe performance of the Caesarean operation." A few days later, another order was circulated explaining the method for preventing infantile paralysis.[3] Dispensation of information by the government proved extremely helpful in 1795 and 1796, when a strange disease known as "seven-day ailment" appeared in San Antonio. The ailment attacked infants on the seventh day with

★

spasms and was usually fatal. A remedy was discovered in Cuba, and adopted by the authorities in Texas with saving effect. It consisted of *aceite de palo*, and was applied to the umbilical cord when cut.[4]

Even the hanging out of one's shingle, in some cases, had to be done according to government regulation. A law compelled "any midwife" to post a "large" sign "over her door" announcing availability "to take care of women's afflictions."[5]

Royal instructions included directions for treating almost all ailments from infantile paralysis to fleabites. This writer has not seen the royal treatment for infantile paralysis; but for jigger fleabites, His Majesty directed rubbing the "ravaged" parts with cold olive oil.[6]

SCIENCE AND SUPERSTITION

In many instances, it would be a matter of speculation to say where superstition ended and science began in the practice of frontier medicine. Among the superstitions that made the treatment of slaves difficult was one concerning calomel—a chemical so severe it might have been a blessing to humanity if the slaves had won out. The Negroes believed that this powder was composed of the bones of dead people ground to powder. The castor oil that followed these "rounds" of torturous "cures," they contended, was extracted from the same bodies that furnished the bones for the calomel.[7]

If Doctor Pedro Lartigue's idea about the cause of bilious fever was not an outright superstition, he left no scientific basis for his findings. In July, 1809, the commandant at Trinidad reported that not a single soldier was available for service due to the fever. The government sent Dr. Lartigue to check on the epidemic. The trees, he announced, were the cause of the malady. The doctor's prescription: cut down all the trees as soon as possible.[8]

Malarial fever was attributed, at one time or another, to about everything imaginable except mosquitoes. Bad air, bad food, overexertion, too much sunshine were high on the list of suspects. A Houston newspaper, in 1843, made this enlightening observation: "It has generally been noticed that fevers are most frequent just after the excitements of the September election." For the health and comfort of the voting public, the paper offered its advice on the subject: ". . . We hope that all will bear this in mind and endeavor to avoid all unnecessary excitement; giving way neither to passion nor intemperance." [9]

The most general treatment for malaria involved the traditional "puke, purge, and bleeding." These harsh treatments were supposed to relieve the patient by depletion.

When bleeding was needed, the barber was usually called in to perform this and other surgical "necessities." Some of the Indian medicine men availed themselves of the scientific learning of the civilized white man, and took postgraduate work in this field. Often, the Spaniards called the redskin medicos to their bedside in the absence of white physicians. The Indian practitioners developed a technique for hurrying up slow leaks in veins. They sucked the wound.[10]

In time, Peruvian bark was administered for malaria. This was a distressing treatment because of the upsetting effects on the patient's stomach and the difficulty in measuring uniform dosage. The ultimate discovery and usage

★

of quinine was one of the greatest boons that ever came to Texas.

At one time, the most dreaded scourge in Texas was smallpox. Brown sugar was considered a treatment for the disease. At least there is record of a Captain José Miguel del Moral, of La Bahia, writing to Governor Munoz stating that he was sending soldiers to San Antonio to purchase brown sugar for the treatment of smallpox.

The first efforts at vaccination against smallpox in Texas were primitive and crude; but anything was to be risked in preference to this dangerous, scarring disease. The first materials sent to the province for vaccination were "a vial of pus and a paper sack of smallpox scabs," along with instructions for the use of the scabs.[11]

During the yellow-fever epidemic in Houston, "every exposed place was inundated with lime, and at night, huge bonfires, composed largely of tar barrels and tar, were burned at the street crossings."[12]

Olmstead observed that although the Americans admitted a great deal of chills and fever, they "seemed to think that the Germans were served about right (in their sicknesses) for living without bacon and eating trash, such as fresh fish and ripe cucumbers!"[13]

A group of Mexican railroad workers were found practicing this preventive measure: When they got their feet wet in cold water, they always wet their heads to prevent illness from getting their feet chilled.[14]

Here is an old "cure" for colds: Give equal parts of hot vinegar and water, to which have been added sugar and butter to taste. There were innumerable ones for croup: Ten drops of kerosene on a teaspoon of sugar; inhaling smoke from pine knots; heating turpentine in a spoon and inhaling the fumes. J. Marvin Hunter, Sr., recalls this treatment for soreness of the chest: "It was relieved by wearing a piece of red flannel over it. Between the chest and the flannel was a plaster composed of the following ingredients: Kerosene, oil, syrup, vinegar, axle grease, turpentine, red pepper, and whatever else could be spared from the pantry or barn." [15]

Here is an old prescription for pneumonia: "Take large cabbage leaves and wilt them over a fire to make them soft, then put the leaves all over the patient's chest, sides and back, wrap a thin cloth around the patient to hold the leaves in place, then pour on vinegar just as hot as the patient can stand it. The sick one will start to sweat right away and the pneumonia will be broken up." [16]

In numerous pioneer reports, onions are referred to as a preventive, but nothing very specific is said about what, or whom, they prevent.

The *Texas State Gazette*, October 16, 1852, carried this report on treatment of tuberculosis: ". . . A residence in a sugar house, during the rolling season, far surpasses any other known means of restoring flesh, strength, and health lost by chronic ailments of the chest, throat or stomach. The rolling season is the harvest, when the canes are cut, the juice extracted and converted into sugar . . . Dr. C. says the vapor is most agreeable and soothing to the lungs and in his own case removed a distressing cough. He stood for hours in the sugar house inhaling the vapor and drinking occasionally a glass of the hot cane juice."

For respiratory ailments, teas seem to have been the main standby. There were so many and varied teas, made from mullen leaves, broom weeds, pepper, etc., one wonders if it may have been simply the liquid that did the good, if any.

Hall's Journal of Health, about 1868, gave these directions for treating a cold: ". . . First, eat nothing; second, go to bed, cover up in a warm room; third, drink as much cold water . . . or as much herb teas 'as one can.' " A rancher's prescription for flu: One quart of whisky and a dozen lemons. Directions: Throw the lemons at a fence post and drink the whisky.

The general preventive, in some circles on the frontier was a bag of asafetida tied onto a string and hung from the neck, locket fashion.

Dr. J. C. Massie, about 1853, wrote one of the first books in Texas, the *Theory and Practice of Medicine*. His treatment for removing a tapeworm, drinking mare's milk, was widely noted. He further recommended for this condition "a decoction of garlic in milk with castor oil and tin filings." [17] (One can understand the potential damage to the worm, but one wonders what it did to the patient!)

Lemon juice was given for diphtheria. Poultices of cranberries were administered for erysipelas. A broth made from the lining of chicken gizzards was used to "cure" nausea. Hay fever victims were told to smoke coffee grounds in a pipe. On the Plains, a highly recommended treatment for hemorrhoids was suppositories of pure salt in a base of buffalo tallow.[18]

Unbalanced diet, exposure, and strenuous labor were doubtless contributing factors to the widespread prevalence of rheumatism on the frontier. There were innumerable prescriptions for this affliction. High on the list were rattlesnake oil, buzzard grease, asparagus. A sting of a bee on the heel also was considered beneficial.[19]

Lack of understanding on the part of patients and their families often gave the practitioner trying hours. Shortly after capsules became available, a doctor gave some to an old settler. Later he brought back the "little glass boxes" emptied, and wanted a remittance on them.

Dr. William W. Wallace gave some capsules to a German farmer for his wife to take. A short time later the man rode up to the doctor's home on a horse in a lather and with plow gear still on, so hurriedly had he taken the horse from the plow in the field. "Mein Gott in Himmel, Doctor, come quick!" he shouted. "Mein vife she swollowed dem little glass pottles und dey are cutting her pelly to pieces." No amount of persuasion could convince the husband that the trouble was merely calomel griping the patient. The doctor had to ride 12 miles to satisfy him.[20]

This clinical report of a doctor regarding backaches appeared in the *San Antonio Daily Herald*, August 5, 1856. The physician reported that some of his patients were relieved of backache by wearing less clothing. The physician stated that a lady who had suffered for years from pains in the back and adjacent regions was "induced to adopt hooped and light skirts instead of the heavy ones . . . After a few weeks she said that she was entirely free of backaches and other uncomfortable feelings. . . . She weighed the skirts formerly worn and those lately adopted; the former weighed over four times as much as the latter. This difference in weight with the greater freedom of movement . . . and oppressive heat about the loins . . . might convince . . . those [suffering] . . . to adopt hooped or light skirts . . ." [21]

The *Texas Nation Register*, March 22, 1845, carried this: "Cure of a Lady's Sore Throat—An improved formula of the distinguished Dr. Onderdonk . . . who disclaims the honor of the invention" but contents himself with the "more humble merit of having tested its infallible virtues by a series of skillful and interesting experiments": "Embrace the neck of the patient closely, yet tenderly, in a gentleman's coat sleeve; and be sure there is an arm in it."

Most of the early remedies were prepared by women in the homes. Pills were made of flour mixed with the boiled inner bark of ash trees for action on the liver and bowels. Willow bark was prepared in the same way for use as a tonic. A brew prepared from green gourds was used as an emetic. Antidotes for snake bites included: gunpowder and vinegar; brandy and salt; alum; a drink made from the bark of the black ash tree; and tobacco juice. Frequently, rattlesnake bite was treated by applying the fleshy part of the tail of the killed snake to the bite to draw out the poison.

Surgery was often of the "kitchen-table" variety. In the early 90's, a saloon keeper of Amarillo, named M. E. ("Mel") Thompson, came down with appendicitis. In view of his appearance and self-treatment, the idea has been ventured that he was an ex-doctor. He was described as a pale, slight, picturesque character who looked more like a country doctor than a bartender. He operated upon himself. He left the incision open for several months, draining the wound from time to time. He recovered.[22]

Noah Smithwick wrote as follows of the doctors in Austin's colony: "The major part of their practice was devoted to the dressing of wounds and holding inquests." [23] He spoke admiringly of one doctor: "He dealt out calomel and quinine with remarkable success." [24]

Smithwick quoted Gail Borden (who, along with other enterprises, practiced medicine) on the subject of treatments: "It is no use to be a doctor unless you put on the airs of one. Nine times out of ten, sickness is caused by overeating or eating unwholesome food; but a patient gets angry if you tell him so; you must humor him. This I do by taking one grain of calomel and dividing it into infinitesimal parts, adding sufficient starch to each part to make one of these little pellets (exhibiting a little vial of tiny white pills), then glaze them over with sugar. In prescribing for a patient, I caution him about his diet, warning him that the pills have calomel in them. Well, the result is that he abstains from hurtful articles of food, which is all he needs to do anyway." [25]

It took a long time for the qualified doctors and the public to weed out the quacks on the frontier. A petition to authorities by a group of Texas doctors, in August, 1835, reflects this condition: ". . . These pseudo M.D.'s or Drs. are, we sincerely believe, more dangerous than the hostile Indians, and not considerably less numerous. Certainly more brave men have fallen under their hands than the rifles of the Caddos, Wacos, Towaccanies, and Comanches ever reached. We had at anytime rather see a company of armed Mexicans in battle array than a squad of these grave gentry, parading with Pandora's boxes in the shape of pill bags . . . dealing damnation round the land by various infernal compounds of mercury, lead, ratsbane, etc. . . . Some of these impostors have acquired the honorable and distinguished title of doctor merely by the simple process of emigration and distinguished by that vast fund of medical knowledge acquired in a livery stable, cook shop, or tan vat; they decide upon the morbid state of the human system . . ." [26]

What the healers lacked in quality they often made up in quantity. A father lamenting the loss of his baby was heard to tell a neighbor: "It was only five months old. We did all we could for it. We had four doctors, blistered its head and feet, put mustard poultices all over it, gave it nine calomel powders, leeched its temples, had it bled, and gave it all kinds of medicines, and yet after a week's illness, it died." [27]

One doctor stated that he always gave his patient "something to make them die easy." [28] There may have been more truth than unintended humor in the answer of a frontier Negro to the question as to what doctor had attended his lately deceased brother: "Bill didn't have no doctah, he died a natural death."

CHAPTER TWELVE

Fightin' Men

INDEPENDENCE IN THE RANKS

Military "formality" never squelched the pioneer Texans' spirit of independence. From the very start, Texans carried their independence into the ranks. Volunteers normally outfitted themselves with arms, ammunition, and provisions; and sometimes with mounts. They elected their captains by majority vote. When candidates were "running" they were placed some distance apart in front of the men. At the word "March" the men fell into line by the side of their favorite. The candidate receiving the most men in his line was declared in command.[1] Under this system an officer held a politician's obligation to his men.

When Captain Andrews retired from the command of the Texas Rangers, he was succeeded by Captain William N. Eastland. The new captain, observing the conduct of the men of the company, decided that his predecessor had been too slack. He promptly announced that some changes would be made to tighten discipline. Whereupon the men, just as promptly, marched out, stacked their

★

arms, and told the new captain to go to hell and they would go home. Eastland had the good sense to yield gracefully to his men, and lived to make his country a valuable officer.[2]

"Accidents" sometimes befell the "upstart" officer who knew more about rules than psychology. Smithwick told of another discipline situation in which a certain Captain H—— "the only officer who ever had the temerity to try to enforce strict military discipline, paid for his folly with his life. There came up a violent thunderstorm one night, and when it was over . . . [he] was found in his tent with his brains blown out."[3]

The usual command among the Rangers for starting an engagement was: "All ready, boys, Go ahead," or "Follow me."

Officers trained in military institutes often looked down their noses at such unorthodox procedure, but confusion due to misunderstanding of orders was negligible. In the grim days of the frontier when fighting was almost everybody's business, a citizen might leave his plow in the middle of a row; and if and when he came back probably hitch up his "cavalry" mount and plow the row out. He did not go to boot camp, technical school, or officers' training school to learn "proper" military language. He did not have the time, for the enemy was nearly always at hand.

The strict officer did not last long on the frontier. Formal parades were rare and generally regarded by the Rangers as a nuisance. A captain of a regiment, shortly after his arrival on the Rio Grande, during the early days of the Mexican War, called his men together and made the following announcement: "I've got orders, boys, to parade the regiment tomorrow morning, at ten o'clock, to be reviewed by General Taylor. I don't know what the devil we ought to do about it, but I reckon we'd better all draw up in a line, and when he comes by give him three cheers."

So the next morning when the general appeared, the command was sounded. "The cheers were given, every man waving his hat, after which he tossed it into the air, or sent it sailing over the general's head, and drawing his revolver, fired five rounds, in a random *feu de joie*, whooping, hallooing, yelling, and making whatever independent demonstrations of respect and welcome he saw fit." [4]

A man's record under fire took precedence over everything—in the opinion of the old-timers—including schooling, social position, and politics. Though General Rusk never assumed any air of superiority over his men, the dignity of his position demanded a staff. So he appointed a couple of "young striplings, sons of old friends," as aides, with the rank of major. "One day a bluff old citizen called on the general, and, being well acquainted with him, walked into his tent without any ceremony, ignoring the presence of the youthful aides until Rusk formally introduced them as 'Major Dexter and Major Hoxie, my aides.'

" 'Aides, h—l!' said the old fellow, looking the boys over contemptuously; 'when I was their size I went in my shirt tail.' " [5]

PRACTICAL SOLDIERS

The frontier soldier lacked polish and discipline, and was notably innocent of military manuals, but he made up the deficiency in what the pioneers admiringly called

★

"guts" and horse sense. He was a practical battler, not a parade artist.

When the early Texans had fighting to do they simply grabbed anything they had handy that might be used to dispatch the enemy—or went to the nearest shop and made something—and started using it as quickly as they could contact the foe.

Noah Smithwick told how he and his company prepared for the Revolution without loss of time: "We brushed the old cannon (an iron six-pounder), scoured it out, and mounted it on an old wooden truck—transverse sections of trees with holes in the centers, into which were inserted wooden axles." Thus was created the famed "Flying Artillery."

"We had no ammunition for our 'artillery,'" Smithwick explained, "so we cut slugs of bar iron and hammered them into balls; ugly-looking missiles they were, I assure you, but destined to 'innocuous desuetude.' . . . We formed a company of lancers and converted all the old files about the place into lances which we mounted on poles cut in the river bottom." [6]

Olmstead quoted this practical arrangement practiced by a Ranger: "As we lay down, Woodland instructed me thus: 'I've got a habit when I go to sleep to take off my Colt always and stick it under the fork of my saddle; then if it rains—'tisn't no matter how hard—there's no danger of it's getting wet, and I know just where 'tis. I always sleep with my head on my saddle, and if I hear anything in the night, I can slide my hand in and get it, without making any rustling, quicker than I could take it out of my belt.'" [7]

Sometimes, on the level Plains, when men were attacked by overwhelming numbers of Indians, and they could find no cover, they killed their mounts and used them for breastworks. This at times served a double purpose, for the smell of horse blood sometimes stampeded the Indians' ponies, at least it usually prevented them from charging in close.[8]

General John B. Hood's life was dramatically saved because a private disobeyed orders. In going into an engagement Hood ordered all rifles to be unloaded—a precaution against indiscriminate firing. As he was riding in front of the Fourth Texas Infantry leading the advance, he suddenly ran into a Federal picket, the corporal of which jumped up and aimed his rifle at him. It looked as if the commander was going to be killed in front of the entire brigade, and nothing could be done about it, for all

★

rifles were unloaded, or supposed to be. At that critical moment, a shot rang out and the Federal corporal fell dead and the Texas commander's life was saved. Private John Deal had been more practical than obedient.[9]

Military uniforms have appealed to fighting Texans, but uniforms were never essential. There was never any "fancy-pants" complex in the Texas ranks. The Texans preferred to wear what they could get into quickest and fight best in. The Texas Rangers, for instance, never adopted any uniform.

When the Bayou City Guards were organized at Houston for Civil War service, T. W. House, Sr., sent them a box of white kid gloves, and the boys paraded up main street with them—but not wearing them on their hands. The members put them on their bayonets. The unit became known as the "Kid Glove Gentry." [10]

Sam Houston thought that fighting men were born, not made in military institutes. He said: "You might as well take dung-hill fowl's eggs and put them in eagles' nests and try to make eagles of them, as to try to make generals of boys who have no capacity, by giving them military training." [11]

According to one old-timer, when the early Texans had battle to do, they "sized up the situation, got as many fighting men together as practical, and without dressing up or reading the rule books went to it."

TEXANS RUSH IN WHERE ANGELS FEAR TO TREAD

The reckless bravery of Texas fighting men is legendary. The "rearin'-to-go" spirit caused blunders, but in fighting savage Indians and bandits, one could not wait for an Act of Congress in order to get started. A great portion

166

of the pioneer population came to this wild country either to get into a fight or mindful of the fact that they would likely be in one, off and on, until the land was won. The faint hearts simply did not come to this wilderness claimed and contested by Indians and Mexicans.

Sam Houston, who was more sympathetic toward the Indians than the average Texan, realized, in time, the futility of trying to prevent the white and red races from fighting each other. He said: "If I could build a wall from the Red River to the Rio Grande, so high that no Indian could scale it, the white people would go crazy trying to devise means to get beyond it." [12]

Eagerness usually overcame any wishy-washiness. In an address on the eve of the Revolution, Stephen F. Austin said: "Retreat is now impossible; we must go forward to victory or die the death of traitors. . . . I will wear myself out by inches rather than submit to Santa Anna's arbitrary rule."

Commentators have remarked that Texans were the best of soldiers in a fight and the worst conceivable in lulls between battles. The eagerness to fight often led to unnecessary loss of life. Smithwick stated that the first freeman's life lost in the Revolution was "recklessly, foolishly" thrown away. The soldier, Dick Andrews, along with some other men were ordered by Bowie, then near San Antonio, to go to the support of Fannin. "Excited and eager to get a shot, some of the boys mounted the bank and cut across, exposed to the fire of the whole Mexican army." [13]

Jefferson Davis addressing Texas soldiers said: "The troops from other states have a reputation to make; you Texans have one to sustain."

The Battle of Antietam illustrated the reckless, stub-

★

born bravery of Texans in the Civil War. James Farber reports: "The First Texas was at eighteen percent of its strength when Antietam was over; the Fourth, at forty-seven percent; and the Fifth, at twenty-five percent." [14]

Independence and recklessness was not limited to the ranks. Practical necessity, as a rule, took precedent over regulations, even among generals.

Few people know that the United States was invaded by a foreign power in 1838, but the incident created quite a stir in Washington. President Van Buren sent an urgent message to the 25th Congress titled "Texas Invasion— Louisiana" containing "Information in relation to the invasion of the Southwestern Frontier by an armed force from the Republic of Texas."

The trouble started when a rebellion broke out among the Mexicans of the Nacogdoches vicinity against the authority of Texas. Several tribes of Indians, including the Caddos, supported the rebels.

General Thomas J. Rusk quickly organized a corps of volunteers, and in short time suppressed the revolt. Once the rebellion was crushed Rusk took up the trail of the Caddos—considered the most dangerous tribe in East Texas. They had relinquished their lands in Northwest Louisiana by treaty; but with Rusk on their trail, they beat a hasty path across the international boundary line to their old stamping grounds. Once Rusk took out after the Caddos he paid about as much attention to the American boundary as the Indians did.

The Caddos did not stop until they reached the heart of Shreveport, and Rusk did not stop until he caught them there. Then and there he took their guns away from them, and had them sign a treaty.

While Rusk was disarming the Caddos, American officials let out a great howl about "violation of our territory . . . and filling a peaceful village with armed soldiery." Officials protested, and sent hurried messages to Washington and to nearby army posts for aid to repulse the invaders who had "threatened the peace of our families, the welfare of the town, and the dignity of the United States." Rusk went right on taking the Caddos' guns and telling them what he would do if he ever caught another Caddo aiming a gun at a Texan.

When the plea for aid reached Colonel Many, commanding officer at Fort Jesup (20 miles east of the Sabine River), he gave orders for every available man in the fort to prepare to march.

The next day he marched off in a great huff with 160 men and one piece of artillery "to arrest General Rusk and his band of Texans and bring them to justice."

This was a tedious and dramatic situation—the prospect of a United States and Texas army locked in a pitched battle.

Though Colonel Many buckled on his sword with great blustering, it seems that he broke no speed record on the march to clash with the Texas Indian fighter. Actually we do not have record of what happened. It would seem that by the time Colonel Many reached Shreveport, if he did, General Rusk had attended to the business he came for, and had gone back to Texas as unconcerned about the boundary as when he came.

The State and Military Departments spread a lot of ink

★

about this "invasion." Actually, however, peaceful citizens on both sides of the border were glad that somebody had the practical initiative to put the warring Indians in their places without delay.[15]

MILITARY ODDITIES

It seems that anything could happen during the varied campaigns conquering and securing this new country. Texas history is replete with military oddities.

The muzzle-loaders of frontier days required paper wads to press the charge close to the shot. Therefore paper wads were essential to the defense of the frontier, and it was usually a scarce commodity. In 1801 the enlarged garrison at San Antonio became depleted of this item. In desperation an ingenious sergeant, with more concern for the immediate safety of the population than for the enlightenment of posterity, proposed that the San Antonio Archives be used for gun wadding. Spanish red tape probably saved the irreplaceable archives from destruction, for regulations decreed that not even scrap paper could be disposed of without the consent of the commanding general, who, in this instance, turned the request down and authorized the purchase of scrap paper in Saltillo.[16]

The entire supply of powder in Texas at the beginning of the Revolution "would scarce have sufficed to charge one of the big guns now [1900] in use," according to Noah Smithwick, who was there and was in a position to know.[17]

Smithwick also reported on the composition of the army: "We soon had more officers than men." [18]

The first Mexican officer to take arms against the Texans in their fight for independence was an American—

170

John D. Bradburn, an adventurer from Kentucky who had gone to Mexico with Mina. In the spring of 1832, he imprisoned several citizens of Anahuac supposedly because of their resistance to his arbitrary acts. Actually, it is claimed that this fight was set off because of a practical joke played upon him.

The defenders of the Alamo fought under a Mexican flag, the flag of the constitution of 1824. Having no other, and being too busy to make another one, the Texans let the Mexican flag fly.

James Bowie, one of the most effective fighters of the Alamo, fought the battle in bed. Recently injured in a fall, and unable to stand, he had his cot moved to a strategic position where he continued to fire until killed.

The town of San Felipe was burned because of a herd of cattle. On March 26, 1836, the inhabitants, seeing a cloud of dust raised by an approaching herd of cattle, thought it was caused by an advancing column of Mexican cavalry. They hastily gathered their movable goods, set fire to the town and fled beyond the Brazos River.

From the Texas point of view, one fine joke on the invading Mexicans occurred, though actually it was at the Texans' expense. At one town the Mexicans gathered up everything of value and stored it carefully before they left, planning to return and possess the land from which they thought they were expelling the Texans for good. The Comanches followed them, and after taking all they wanted, set fire to the town.

One unit of soldiers marching to San Jacinto was "routed" by a drove of cattle, and as a result missed the famous battle. In the Brazos bottom, scouts discovered in the moonlight a large body of moving objects coming down the road. This was taken to be Gaona's division of the Mexican Army. The men detoured up the river to make a crossing and consequently arrived at San Jacinto a day late to learn of victory and the army of cows.

The Texas Rangers quickly made a reputation for accomplishing the extraordinary. One of their first official acts was to capture three Mexican ships at sea. Twenty Rangers overhauled a small boat sent to shore from a Mexican ship. Sixteen of them got in, rowed back to the ship, captured it, and waited for two other Mexican ships to come alongside and then captured both of them. They became known as the "Horse Marines."

The Battle of San Jacinto regarded as sixteenth in importance among the world's battles (Waterloo was fifteenth) lasted only 18 minutes. It secured the freedom of Texas, and decided the fate of a million square miles of territory.

There was a complete rout of the Texans following the Battle of San Jacinto, and not a shot was fired at them. According to one observer: "The arms and ammunition captured were brought into camp. No one wanted the muskets, so they were stacked; and, as the cartridges wouldn't fit our guns, they were thrown into a heap. By some means fire got among them (the cartridges) and there was a stampede, such as they never could have created shot from muskets in the hands of the Mexicans. 'Pop! Fizz! Bang!' The enemy was charging every point of the compass! The air was full of bursting shells. The proud victors of San Jacinto dropped their guns and fled.

Trees were at a premium. The blind enemy held the camp until the last cartridge was exhausted." [19]

Everything about Santa Anna, the Mexican general, was as false as he intended his promises to be. His saddle fairly glittered with gold, which he said was solid and valued at $600, but it was found later to be only plated. The magnificent black stallion he was riding was stolen property.

The military booty at San Jacinto amounted to $9.75 per man. The spoils were sold at auction and prorated among the participants in the battle.[20]

At the Battle of Monterey, so the story goes, a group of Texas Rangers stormed a battery on foot, fighting with Bowie knives. The Rangers helped take the town; but several regiments of volunteers were required to take them— out of town, that is, because of the riot they were causing in the process of celebrating their victory.[21]

The first general order supposedly issued by Robert E. Lee in Texas was a strange, but welcomed, one. It proclaimed that no longer could hot branding irons be applied to United States soldiers for minor breaches of discipline.[22]

During the Civil War, powder makers used bat guano as a source of gunpowder. They secured the guano from smelly, bat-inhabited caves and put it in wood or stone hoppers. On top of a layer of guano, they placed pads of broom straw, and on top of this a layer of wood ashes. They poured water on top and filtered it into cast-iron boilers beneath. The boilers were heated and, at the proper time, the liquid was poured into vats. There, saltpeter—the vitally needed ingredient for gunpowder—was crystallized

★

by evaporation. It was then sacked for shipment to a powder mill.[23]

GUNPOWDER AND LAUGHTER

Few Texans have ever been too busy, whether at war or peace, to stop for a laugh or to create one. They have frequently shown that even war can have its lighter moments. Texas Ranger Big Foot Wallace had to call a fellow Ranger to task on a matter of military ethics. Wallace was shooting at an Indian running up a hill when his colleague came along and prepared to take a shot at the fleeing target. "Get away," ordered Wallace sharply. "This is my Indian. Go find an Indian of your own."

Sometimes haste and lack of precautions lost the day. Noah Smithwick told of a battle lost amid much laughter and cursing. Martin De Leon had lost much stock to the Cronks by constant raids. He determined to take matters into his own hands. He organized his retainers into an army, and mounting a four-pounder swivel gun on a jackass, set out to annihilate the tribe. He ran the Indians to cover, brought his artillery to bear and touched it off, "but he did not take the precaution to brace up the jackass, and the recoil turned him a flying somersault, landing him on top of the gun with his feet in the air, a position from which he was unable to extract himself. The Mexicans got around him and tried to boost him, but the jackass had had enough of that kind of fun and philosophically declined to rise until released from his burden, so they had to dismount the jackass. By that time the Indians had disappeared." [24]

The Karankawas and the Tonkawas pestered Captain

Aylett C. "Strap" Buckner almost constantly. Finally he decided he had had enough of it, and concocted a scheme to rid himself of both tribes. He encouraged a spat going on between the tribes.

As expected, representatives of the Karankawas came to his store saying that they could make short work of their enemy if Buckner would furnish them arms and ammunition. Buckner complied with their request. Soon the Tonkawas came with the same plea for assistance, and the obliging Buckner fitted them out for battle.

On the day of battle, Buckner repaired to the field of conflict, an open prairie, and at a safe distance, with field glasses, viewed the operations he hoped would completely exterminate the Indians. Warriors of the two tribes rushed out of a belt of timber from opposite sides of the prairie, yelling at each other, and opened fire before they were within shooting distance. Much to Buckner's disgust, they wasted all their ammunition without wounding a single Indian.[25]

General Mackenzie had been warned that it would be impractical to take any type of wheeled vehicle into Palo Duro Canyon on an Indian campaign. So he had two Howitzers mounted on the back of two big American mules.

Later, when he found his men close pressed by the enemy, who were hidden from view behind rocks and brush, he ordered his mule battery into action. The soldiers turned the mules around into position, tail foremost, and discharged the cannons. The volley was a notable success—but not in the manner the general had expected. At the first fire of the cannons, the husky animals stampeded and "tore around at a marvelous rate. They ran into the

★

Indians' line, tore through them, and finally headed back to the general's command.

The superstitious Indians were so demoralized, they too stampeded. Some members of the band later told American officers that they had faced all kinds of guns carried by the white man without fear, but when it came to shooting mules at them they had to run.[26]

The military retort supreme was made by Sam Houston to Santa Anna when the captured Mexican general asked him: "Why didn't you attack me yesterday before General Cos came up?"

"Oh, I didn't think it worth while to make two bites of a cherry," Houston answered.

To avoid rumors and leaks of information to the enemy, Stonewall Jackson issued strict orders that soldiers "know nothing" when questioned about military matters. One day he came upon a Texan who was leaving his squad to pluck some ripe cherries. He was accosted by the general, who asked: "Where are you going?"

"I don't know," the Texan answered.

"What is your regiment?"

"I don't know."

"Well what do you know?"

"I don't know nawthin'."

"Well, why do you always answer 'I don't know?'"

"Because them's o' Stonewall Jackson's orders, an' I'm a-goin' to obey 'em or bust!"

"Is that all you know?"

"No, I know I want some of them cherries."

"Go on and get them." [27]

During the Civil War, officers often wore no insignia.

This confusing practice frequently led to unorthodox incidents. General B. F. Cheatham was riding along a road near Cumberland Gap one day when a skinny, half-starved Texan espied the eight or ten ears of corn that were tied to the general's saddle. The Texan stopped him.

"Old man," the boy began, "I'll give you a dollar apiece for them ears of corn."

The general drew himself up and stared at the lad for a moment. "Do you know who I am?" he asked.

"No," replied the Texan, "and I don't give a damn, but I'll do what I said about that corn."

He got the corn.[28]

CHAPTER THIRTEEN

Laws and Lawyers

SPANISH LAWS

The laws of Spanish Texas were, in the main, severe and tedious. A cattle thief received much more publicity than a murderer does now. When a suspect was convicted of stealing cattle, the paunch and entrails of a steer, recently slaughtered, were obtained and tied around his neck. Thus encumbered with his gory burden, the offender was forced to walk up and down the main street before the jeering, booing mob. This punishment evidently was more effective than present-day penalties, for records of repeat offenders are practically nonexistent.[1]

A person convicted of murder or witchcraft could, according to law, be quartered alive. Perjury carried a sentence of ten years at hard labor in the galleys. Vagrants were subject to 60 lashes on the bare back. Prostitutes were banished one year for each offense.[2]

The Spaniards used imagination in making laws: "Any man who shall consent to the prostitution of his wife, for the first offense, shall be exposed in public. He shall then be rubbed with honey and feathered. He shall then be made to wear a fool's cap, a string of garlic around his neck, and a pair of horns on his head. He shall then be given 100 lashes and then sent to the galleys for ten years. For the second offense he shall be sent to the galleys for life." [3]

One Spanish law was inspired by the frailty of mankind in handling public funds. A chest containing public money was required to have three locks. Three different officials carried the keys, often the governor and *alcaldes*. When funds were deposited or withdrawn all three officials had to be present, each to open his respective lock—and to watch the other's hand when it dipped into the treasury.

Nacogdoches probably enacted the first Texas city ordinances concerning traffic lights. Long before the province became a republic, any pedestrian who failed to carry a lantern while walking in the street at night was subject to one week in jail. [4]

In June, 1809, a law was passed in San Antonio making the act of riding double and galloping down main street on festive days a misdemeanor punishable by a fine of five pesos and ten days in jail. Too enthusiastic celebrating on holidays had caused an alarming number of accidents. [5]

The Laws of the Indies, for many years, made it a capital offense for any foreigner to enter the colony without a special license from the king. Permission to travel was not granted unless research in natural history was the ostensible object. Thus, most American filibusters, when encountered in Spanish Texas by officials of His Majesty's Government, were found observing the birds and the flowers. A queer sort of procedure, but it was grounds for argument.

★

It gave the local Spanish officials an opportunity to show leniency when they felt like it.

The chief cause of increasing suspicion among the Spaniards toward exploring naturalists was their attachment for wild horses—which very often formed the bulk of their "collections." These "scholars" frequently developed a hobby of trading among the tribes and as a result many were carried into the interior in chains.

In the early days there was not so great a danger of a man losing his freedom, but any number of offenses might lead to a broken neck. The following crimes were punishable by hanging during Spanish days: Incest, manslaughter, dueling, sodomy, the theft of 12 or more goats, the theft of five hogs, rape, and treason. At least 14 offenses were made punishable by death under acts of Congress passed late in 1836.[6] Part of the explanation for this emphasis on the death penalty: Prisons were scarce, insecure, and expensive. There were plenty of trees.

In 1807 a law was passed prohibiting the Indians from speaking their native tongue. They were "required" to speak Spanish only, in order that they might learn to communicate more easily and freely with the Spaniards.[7]

Open fires were prohibited. A fine of three pesos was imposed upon any citizen convicted of burning trash. This might be considered as a signal to Indians.[8]

Government permission had to be secured before a person could slaughter a hog or beef for home use. A private or public dance could not be given without a permit. It was stated by statute who could bake bread for public use.[9]

Almost a century before the coming of the automobile, the city of San Antonio inaugurated the parking meter idea into law. Beginning in January, 1809, riders and muleteers were charged 25 cents for the privilege of hitching their mounts and beasts of burden. Even then, the hitching zone was restricted to the area behind the church on the main plaza. One convicted of hitching elsewhere was fined two pesos.[10]

The same year, the city councilmen passed a law prohibiting a man and woman riding the same horse. The practice was considered indecorous.

Possibly the law placing some men in the most helpless position was one that held husbands "accountable for wives out after curfew." [11]

AMERICAN LAWS

During the days of American colonization, the laws provided that two single men might constitute a family for colonization purposes. Many of the so-called 300 families consisted of a *couple* of "old bachelors." [12]

After 1836, laws in Texas went through a rapid transformation: First the Legislature of the Republic overhauled them; then in 1846 the constitution and statutes of the American Congress took effect.

With the advent of trains, traffic became "rapid, reckless and dangerous." In 1853, the legislature required locomotives to be equipped with bells of at least 30 pounds weight; and the bells were required to be sounded continuously as an alarm, beginning at least 80 rods before reaching any crossing. It was made illegal for any engineer to sit at the throttle while intoxicated.

A movement toward more purity and respectability was in the air in 1873: that year the city council of El Paso

★

made it illegal to swim naked in the acequias of the city.

In 1882 the Texas legislature levied a tax of $500 per year upon any person or firm selling either the *Police Gazette* or the *Police News* within state limits. Apparently, the solons considered these stories of crime too exciting for this country of quick-trigger individuals.

This legislature, it appears, began work in earnest to tame the country. It imposed a tax of $500 on public fights between men and bulls, bears, or dogs. As if to make a clean sweep, it levied heavy license fees ranging from $175 to $500 upon patent-medicine drummers, fortunetellers, cockfighters, and clairvoyants.

According to the unwritten law of the range country, a bona fide traveler could enter a house in the absence of the owner and, so long as he took only food required for immediate needs, he was not a burglar. No ranch houses were locked.

One of the strangest, most ironical legal opinions in Texas was rendered by the attorney general in May, 1900, to the effect that a Texas Ranger (other than an officer) had no authority to execute criminal process or make arrest. Any private or noncommissioned officer who arrested a criminal was guilty of false imprisonment and subject to arrest and prosecution. The interpretation, in reality, destroyed the Texas Rangers until the legislature could meet and amend the law.

One of the first ordinances passed by the city council of Amarillo prohibited sleeping in basements. Why this dry-aired community passed such a law is particularly puzzling in view of the fact that there was not a single basement in the town, so far as anyone knows.[13]

On June 12, 1902, the council established by statute the fare that hack drivers could charge: "For calls anywhere in the city limits, 25 cents. When hack has to wait for one to dress, price 50 cents." [14]

In 1892 the council passed a law that made the male population of Amarillo be particular about whom they were found riding with. It became a violation of the law for any man to be seen in a vehicle with a certain class of the opposite sex between the hours of 4 A.M. and 9 P.M. [15]

SHENANIGANS IN THE COURTHOUSE

Possibly mankind is never so ingenious as when his freedom or property is at stake. In some cases, native chicanery proved of greater value than legal learning: An old-timer from the backwoods was tried on a charge of hog stealing. He had no money to employ an attorney. He declined to have one furnished by the state.

The prosecuting attorney put on his witnesses and examined them, and then turned them over to the defendant for questioning. He did not ask a single question.

When instructed to produce his witnesses, he said that he had none. After the attorney closed his argument, the defendant was invited to make a speech. He declined. He did, however, ask permission to whisper a word or two to each of the jurors. This was granted.

After he spoke to them, the jurors marched out.

Within a few minutes they brought in a verdict of "not guilty."

The verdict was so contrary to law and evidence that it amazed everyone present. Outside, the attorney explained to the defendant that he was free and could not be tried

★

again. He would give him ten dollars if he would tell him what he had whispered in the ears of the jurors.

The old-timer reached for the ten, and replied: "I said, 'Now is the time for all us hog thieves to hang together!' " [16]

After a civil case had been argued in central Texas, and taken under advisement by the judge, upon leaving the courtroom one of the parties said to his lawyer: "I think I'll send the judge a box of cigars."

"That would never do!" replied the lawyer quickly. "He would take that as an attempt to bribe him. He would surely decide against you! If he decides in your favor, then you can send him the cigars."

A few weeks later the lawyer met his client on the street and congratulated him on winning his case. "Now you can send the judge a box of cigars."

"I sent them the next day after the trial," the client replied.

"I told you not to do that," the attorney stormed. "It's a wonder he didn't decide the case against you."

The client replied quickly: "But I put my opponent's name in the box." [17]

Some people contend that a paid lawyer is justified in pulling any trick to win a case for his client.

A hardly believable but much enjoyed story is told about a wealthy cattleman who shot a man to death in a Panhandle town. He immediately telegraphed a leading criminal lawyer in Fort Worth, 300 miles away, offering him a fee of $5,000 to defend him.

The lawyer wired back: "I'm leaving for your town on next train; bringing three eyewitnesses."

Sometimes lawyers have been too smart for their own good. The story is told of one attorney pleading a case he thought hopeless. He managed to slip a note to one of the jurors of questionable integrity: "$100 for a verdict of manslaughter."

The jury retired, and after several hours brought in the wished-for verdict of manslaughter.

Next day the juror came to the lawyer's office for his pay-off.

"Good work," the lawyer commended him. "You must have had considerable trouble bringing some of them around—it took you so long."

"I had a lot of trouble," replied the ex-juror. "I thought for a while they were going to acquit the defendant in spite of all I could do."

Judge Roy Bean used an amazing combination of bluff, luck, and common sense to ride legal herd over the country west of the Pecos. The loopholes he found in the law were extraordinary holes indeed. One day a friend of his was brought before his bar of "justice" in the Jersey Lily Saloon charged with carrying a concealed weapon.

"The charge won't stick," the judge pronounced. "If he was standing still when he was arrested he wasn't carrying a weapon because he wasn't going no place; and if he was not standing still he was traveling, and it's legal for travelers to carry weapons. Case dismissed."

Doubtless Roy learned some tricks in his early days when he was a defendant. One night, so the story goes, he came home in a very bad humor with his wife, who had already gone to bed. A heated argument started, and Roy flew into a rage, snatched a burning stick from the fire-

★

place, jerked the covers off the bed, and applied the fiery end of the stick to his wife's anatomy. She fled from the house screaming, and did not stop until she got home to her mother.

When she was able to get about without discomfort she filed suit for aggravated assault.

In court the case went hard against Roy—until the closing argument when his council requested the plaintiff to show the jury the scars which she alleged she had received.

She hesitated, and finally refused. The judge lost patience and dismissed the case.

Outside the courtroom, Roy took his attorney to task. "Why did you take a chance like that? If the jury had seen those scars I might never have got out of jail!"

"I didn't take much of a chance," the lawyer answered. "You ought to know that a Mexican woman wouldn't let a stranger look at her ankles if she could help it. I knew that she wouldn't lift her dress before that bunch of men." [18]

★

CHAPTER FOURTEEN

The Texas Language

PICTURESQUE SPEECH

Ingenuity and originality are vividly revealed in the utterances of unsophisticated, practical men taming a wilderness in a hurry. Secretary of War Thomas J. Rusk outlined to President Burnet's Cabinet the strategy Texans should follow against Santa Anna: "We are in a helluva fix. . . . Let's go to the saloon, have a stiff drink, and fight our way out of it." That is exactly what the Texans did . . . which is, in brief, the story of the Revolution.

Martin Palmer, a 75-year-old soldier, a bowie knife in his hand, was found stalking among the routed Mexicans after San Jacinto, looking for Santa Anna. "When I find him, I'm cutting myself a razor strop, right out of the middle of his back," he explained.

A subtle expression of ambition by Sam Houston proved a prophecy. According to this story, while on his way to Texas, Houston accepted a razor as a gift from a man in Arkansas with the remark:

★

"I accept your gift, my friend, and, mark my words, if I have any luck this blade will some day shave the chin of the president of a republic."

To the people of early Texas, greatness meant:

"A man who was careful of his clothes, didn't drink spirits, could read the Bible without spelling the words, and could eat a cold dinner on washday to save the wimminfolks the trouble of cooking."

Everyone accepted such dictums as:

"None came West save for health, wealth, or a ruined reputation."

"Colonel Colt made all men equal."

Instructions given to beginning scouts:

"Scouts tie their scalps to their brains. Anybody who flunks in this school, in which the Indians conduct the examinations, is scalped."

Advice to the horse buyer:

> One white foot, *buy* him.
>
> Two white feet, *try* him.
>
> Three white feet, *deny* him.
>
> Four white feet and white nose,
>
> Cut off his head and throw him to the crows.

A cowboy's description of himself:

"He could eat centipedes for breakfast and barbed wire for supper without injuring his digestion; and ride all day and dance all night without missing a step." [1]

The ultimate in abstinence:

"Sober as a watched Puritan." If one did not remain sober, the next morning one might feel:

"Like the frazzled end of a misspent life."

Explanation for a weak or runty calf:

"Knocked in the head with the churn dasher."

Expression of Indian slightly wounded:

"Proud, heap proud; white man miss so close." [2]

Comment on old Enfield muskets, known for their powerful kick:

"They would get meat at both ends."

Expression of time of day:

"The sun was about cordwood high."

The man who knew too much to suit his neighbors:

"So swell-headed he couldn't put on his hat without using a shoehorn."

A simile used by the pious who objected to dancing:

"Thick as fiddlers in hell."

A simile used by restless outdoorsmen, such as David Crockett:

"Long as a rainy Sunday."

A well-understood comparison used by frontier chicken raisers:

"Busy as a coon in a hen roost."

A Texas compliment:

"You're mighty Confederate."

Description of a Texas Ranger:

"He could ride like a Comanche, shoot like a Tennesseean, and fight like the devil."

Report of a Ranger (an example of the understatement):

"We had a little shooting, and he lost."

Many of the colorful words and phrases of the frontier have survived: "Telling a windy" means relating a tall

★

tale. "Pulling a sandy" means putting something over on somebody. "Sweating a game" means being a spectator at a card game. "Staying out with the dry cattle" indicates a man has made a night of it. A man quick at retort has a "good come-back." A physically nervous man is "goosy." A man uninformed on a subject knows about as much about it as "a hog does about Sunday."

When he has had experience he "has taken a little more hair off the dog." A man cold from damp or freezing weather is said to be as cold as "a welldigger in Montana."

A hound is a "pot licker," an argument a "cussfight," and a funeral a "burying."

Ranching produced a vocabulary all its own. The owner is usually called the "Big Boss," his right-hand man probably the "straw boss," "top screw," or "top waddy." An ordinary cowboy is a "waddy," "screw," "buckaroo," or "cowpuncher." To determine the age of an animal, the rancher "tooths" him—that is, he makes an examination of the teeth.

OLD SAWS

Concerning those who came West to the frontier: "The cowards never started, and all the weak died on the road."

"Texas was fine for men and dogs, but hell on women and horses."

"When a bad man dies he goes either to hell or to the Pecos."

Axiom of the cow country: "A man on foot is no man at all."

Cattleman Bob Beverley, of the great virgin cattle country: "It belonged to God and man, instead of the Federal Land Bank and the tax collector."

Will Rogers in a speech to Texas Old-Time Trail Drivers Association: "I wish I could have lived my whole life and drank out of a gourd instead of a paper envelope."

Said of a cowboy pitting his luck against the professional gambler:

"He didn't have no more show than a stump-tailed bull in fly time."

"Never speak of ropes in the house of a man whose father was hanged."

An observation: "The rich get richer and the poor get children."

Range-saying about what a man needed in the early West to get a start:

"A rope, a running iron, and the nerve to use it."

FAMOUS SAYINGS

Many gems of wisdom are found among the mottoes and slogans of noted Texans:

Colonel Barnard E. Bee's observation on Santa Anna's attitude and consequent rout at San Jacinto:

"It's a dangerous thing to despise your enemy."

David Crockett's motto:

"Be sure you are right; then go ahead."

Old frontier saying, used by the Reverend Z. M. Morrell in a speech:

"Never try to influence a man against his inclination when he is hungry."

General Zachary Taylor, often accused of being a Texas hater:

★

"Texans are neither cowards nor gentlemen."

Ranger Bill McDonald:

"No man in the wrong can stand up against a fellow that's right and keep a-coming."

Ranger Jeff Milton expressed the grimness of the rough frontier:

"I never killed a man who didn't need killing."

Big Foot Wallace:

"Never refuse to eat or sleep when you are on the Plains."

General McKenzie (concerning ridding the Plains of raiding Comanches):

"Kill all the nits and you will have no lice." This started the practice among his soldiers of killing women and children along with the men.

Ranch motto:

"Thankful for a rain or a calf any time."

Governor Joseph D. Sayers:

"A Texas governor has only two happy days: the day he is inaugurated and the day he retires."

Saying attributed to Republican gubernatorial candidate Webster Flannagan in 1890:

"What are we here for if not the spoils?"

Governor Roberts:

"Texas may go to hell, but if she does she will go according to law."

A rugged individualist, whose name is not known:

"Let's keep this country where every man is entitled to scratch his own itch."

Wyatt Earp said:

"The most dangerous mob in the world is a leaderless

one, for the reason that there is no one on whom you can pin anything."

Artemus Ward's reaction to Texas tall tales:

"The trouble with Texans is that they know so many things which ain't so."

QUICK ON THE VERBAL DRAW

Texans early became noted for quickness on the draw with a six-shooter. They were also quick and apt at repartee:

When Elizabeth Ney's statues of Austin and Houston were placed in the Hall of Fame at Washington, the curator complained that the works did not place well, that, among other things, Sam Houston towered six feet two.

Miss Ney wrote him:

"If I am correctly informed, God made the two men. I merely reproduced their likenesses. If you are dissatisfied about them, you should take the matter up with God." [3]

A pious sister accosted a wobbly cowboy, well along in his cups:

"What are you going to do when you approach the Lord with whisky on your breath?" [4]

The cowhand steadied himself a moment, then said: "Lady, when I approach the Lord, I'm going to leave my breath here."

S. B. Burnett, cattle baron of 6666 fame, dropped into a wholesale grocery house to buy supplies for his ranch. He handed a list to a young clerk, who did not recognize him. The clerk noted that the list called for, among other items, 100 cases of corn and 100 cases of tomatoes. Noting that the order was running into a large figure, the clerk asked Burnett:

"How much of this stuff can you pay for?"

The cattleman answered bluntly:

"A damn sight more than I'm going to buy."

A traveler became lost in a backwoods settlement and, finding a farm lad, asked him how far it was to the next town.

"I don't know," the boy answered.

The traveler asked several other questions, to which the lad answered, "I don't know."

Finally the stranger said in disgust: "You don't know much, do you?"

"I ain't lost," the boy said.

Ranger Captain Bill McDonald got into an argument with some New York peace officers who insisted that their .38 pistols were as good as the .45's used by the Rangers, that these guns would also kill a man. McDonald replied:

"Yes, if you give him a week to die in."

One of the widest circulated comments about Texas was General Sherman's statement:

"If I owned both Hell and Texas, I would rent out Texas and live in Hell." To which a Texan replied:

"That's right, general, every man for his own country."

LETTERS

When frontier Texans "took pen in hand," they seldom were encumbered by rules of grammar or formal etiquette. Many of their letters have a characteristic flavor.

Justice of the Peace Roy Bean penned one of the most succinct "state papers" on record in response to Governor

Hogg's complaint that he had not turned over to the state its share of the fees he had collected. It read:

> *Dear Governor:*
>
> You run things up in Austin and I'll run 'em down here.
>
> Yours truly,
> *Roy Bean*

That was the end of the matter, except the great laugh that was heard over Texas.

A banker, newly arrived in Texas and unfamiliar with cattlemen and their problems, refused to accept a borrower's explanation that his cattle were poor and there was no sale for them; and that he would have to wait until fall when his cattle were fat and could be sold. The banker wrote: "Unless I receive a check in full payment by return mail, I will proceed to file suit and take judgment against you."

The old-time cowman turned the letter over and wrote on the back:

> *Dear Mr. Banker:*
>
> If you ain't better prepared to meet your God than I am to meet this obligation, you shore are going to hell.
>
> *Yours truly,*[5]

During the "barbed-wire war," some wire-cutters destroyed a fence belonging to a rancher named Foote, in Tom Green County, and ran off with some of his short-

★

horn cattle, including a fine bull. The next morning Mr.
Foote found a note nailed to his front gate:

"If your bull you would hunt for, then call at the first
ranch this side of hell and brand him when you get him."

From the Spanish point of view, the Indian was entitled
to no property rights. He definitely had to look to Heaven
for his reward. The Spanish policy was: Salvation for all,
land for none.

Here is a letter by Richard Fields, a chief of the Chero-
kees, who were late-comers to Texas:

> To Subsprem Governor of Province of Spain,
> *Feburey the fust Day, 1822.*
>
> Dieor Sur I wish to fall down at your feet and
> omblay ask you what must be Dun with us pur
> Indians. We have som Grants that was given us
> when we live under the Spanish Government and
> we wish you to send us news by next mal whether
> tha will be reberst or not and if wer committed we
> will com as soon as possible to present ourselves be-
> fore you in a manner agreeable to our talents, etc.

Some men took advantage of the Indians' illiteracy by
writing derogatory letters of "recommendation" that the
Indians could not read. One Plains Indian went about, for
a time, with a piece of wrinkled paper, which he would
present as an introduction with the statement: "Me heap
good Injun." The letter ran thus: [6]

"The name of this noble red man is Hunkydori. He is
of poor but pious parents. What he wouldn't steal a hound
pup wouldn't pull out of a tan-yard. Red-hot stoves are
supposed to be safe in his presence."

A rancher named Peacock, mainly as a joke, wrote the following letter of "recommendation" for Chief Satank.

"This is Satank, the biggest liar, beggar, and thief on the Plains. What he can't beg of you he will steal. Kick him out of your camp, as he is a lazy good-for-nothing Indian." After a few cool receptions, Satank had a friend read the letter, and then shot Peacock to death.[7]

FUNERAL ORATORY

Charlie Reed was killed when his horse fell during a roundup on the Mexquite Ranch on the Pecos.

Pony Bill, "the Cowboy Preacher," delivered the funeral sermon two days later. It was as Texan as longhorns and tall grass:

> Day afore yesterday this poor, dead boy here throwed on his saddle an' rode out with you in

★

joyous spirits, singin' the songs o' the ranges. Little
did he then dream that he was ridin' right into the
bog of eternity! While cuttin' a steer out o' the
bunch, his hoss struck a prairie-dog hole an' fell,
crushin' poor Charlie to the groun' an' when you
picked 'im up his immortal soul had crossed into
the Great Ranges beyond, from which there ain't
no back trails. Death loves a shinin' mark, an' it
never pitched a rope to a brighter boy.

". . . I say a squarer boy never swung a rope.
No one ever asked a favor of Charlie Reed without it bein' cheerfully granted. He war' never
known to make a low-down play. He never made
a back-set on duty w'en the foreman ordered a ride.
True, he war' wild an' reckless, but thar' war' no
devil-brand wickedness in his make-up. His heart
war' a livin' spring, from which the pure waters o'
friendship an' generosity to'ards his companions o'
the saddle flowed. He could laugh with you over
your joys, an' cuss with you over your sorrow. His
soul seemed to be a blazin' fire o' sympathy, to
wich all who war' chilled by the blasts o' trouble
could come an' warm up.

He war' brave as a lion, but his heart war' as
tender as a Christian woman's. He would fight
like a riled steer fur himself or fur a friend, yet a
little child could take 'im by the hand an' lead him
out of a muss. He warn't a bad man. Did you
notice that on the evening's o' pay he never j'ined
you in your songs an' stories an' fun-making at the
ranch? He'd git up in a corner and sit thar' writin'
page after page, with a look on his face as tender
as ever sot on the face of an angel. He seemed to
never hear your hilarity, but 'd sit thar' an' write,
now an' then wipin' tears from his cheeks on the
back o' 'is hand. Nex' mornin' he'd jump a hoss an'
ride to the post-office; an' what did he do thar? Jus'
an even half o' his month's pay 'd go into a money

order, an' the order 'd be put in an envelope, with
all the sheets o' writin' he writ the night afore, and
then . . . drap it into the box an' walk out with
the purtiest look on his face I ever saw.

Who war' that letter addressed to? To his ol'
widder mother back in the States. Would a bad
man act that way? I tell you boys, Charlie warn't
a reg'larly branded and earmarked church Christian; but I b'lieve when the good Lord saw his
soul a'comin' up the slope day afore yesterday He
throwed down the bars an' let the boy into the
Heavenly Corral with a welcomin' smile. I know
He did; an' I tell you right now, if I found myself tied to a church or a sect as didn't believe as
white a boy as 'im 'd get into Heaven 'thout the
church brand, I'd take a run on the rope an' break
it an' get with a bunch o' Christians that could look
over the corral fence 'ithout first puttin' on the
orthodox specs.

. . . Boys, as you come up to take a last look
. . . an' say goodby to your ol' pardner, I hope
you'll do some serious thinkin'. None o' you knows
who'll be the next. Even now, the pale rider o'
death may be lookin' you over, and takin' down his
rope for a final throw; an' you don't know over
whose head the tug'll fall. I'm afeared none o'
you'd fare as well as Charlie has if you war' run
afore the Heavenly Inspector today. Some o' you
think no more o' breakin' the Commandments o'
God than you do o' breakin' a bronco, an' if you
war' bunched now and started on the Last Drive,
you'd leave the trail to Glory away off to the right.

"Perhaps thar ain't one o' you but thinks he'll
call a halt on six some day, but in the most o' your
cases I'm afeared Gabriel'll git in his call ahead o'
you. Why can't you jar loose from your sins now
an' not keep standin' the Lord off from day to day?
You'll break the strands of His rope o' forebear-

★

ance after awhile, an' hit the bottomless bog o'
damnation with both feet an' sink to eternal misery.
The fences o' sin ain't high, an' you kin jump 'em.
Let me implore you . . . when you stand over
Charlie here . . . each one o' you make a promise
to him that you'll take the trail to Heaven today,
an' foller it in spite o' all allurements the devil
sets up on the cross trails along the road." [8]

MONICKERS

In the early days when people from all over the
world were rushing into Texas for every known reason, it
was the custom never to ask a stranger his name. Rather,
one politely inquired: "What do you want to be called?"

There was no bureau of vital statistics to record births
along with full names, and the population was so new and
changed so rapidly there was not sufficient time to check a
man's references. His appearance, possessions, habits, manners, or profession usually suggested a tag for him.

This practice was applied to both the famous and the in-
famous. Erasmas Smith was just another Smith; but
"Deaf" Smith became a household word. Few people
knew that Big Foot Wallace's real name was William A.[9]

Wallace was not without imagination in thinking up
names. He gave his rifle the tender title of "Sweet Lips."
His hunting knife he referred to as "Old Butcher." He
named his dog "Comanche."

Even assuming the dignified position of governor did
not necessarily exempt one from a nickname. Governor
Ireland was known as "Ox-Cart John" because he preferred ox carts to railroads and had been elected on that
platform.

Judge R. M. Williamson, one of Texas' most colorful and popular judges, was known as "Three-Legged Willie" because one of his legs was useless from the knee down and he strapped it behind him and walked on a wooden leg.

Possibly few people knew that the noted Armenian camel driver employed during the camel experiment in Texas was named Hadji Ali. He was called "Hi-Jolly," because that was about as near as anyone could pronounce it.[10]

"Dog" Kelly, Mayor of Dodge City, and known to every early Texas trail driver, was so called because of his love of dog breeding and racing. "Bat" Masterson, also known to all trail drivers, reputedly gained his nickname by using his walking stick to bat down offenders.[11] "Mustache" Jack was so named for his enormous mustaches. "Honey" Allen earned his name while gathering wild honey and pecans on the Devil's River in 1866.

Unusual occupations were almost sure to bring a monicker: "Varmint" Williams captured wild animals and sold them to a museum in the United States. "Wild Horse" Charley rounded up wild horses. "Beaver Trap" Smith naturally was a trapper. "Mustang" Brown had rounded up and tamed a drove of wild horses.

Physical characteristics or experiences often tagged people. "Waco" Brown had been captured by the Waco Indians. "Sheep" Brown owned many sheep. Men not endowed with physical strength might be christened "Runt," "Nubbin," "Cricket," "Rabbit," "Squirrel," or the like.

Personal possessions were responsible for many titles: Domestic animals were so scarce in Austin's colony that the ownership of a cow by William Cooper gave him the sobriquet of "Cow Cooper." Robert Mitchell, one of the first colonists to raise hogs, was known as "Hog" Mitchell. "Pop Corn" Robinson was so designated because he bought a large corn field near Brazoria.

Appellations were not always complimentary or agreeable to the designees. "Dog" Brown was so called because he reputedly stole someone's dog. A resident of De Witt's colony, who had a few white spots in an otherwise ruddy complexion, was referred to as "Old Paint." "One-Eyed" Wallace lost an eye in an Indian fight. "Sawmill" Cooper was mangled in a sawmill accident.

Conspicuous habits, particularly unpopular ones, brought tags: Robert Williams wore store clothes and was called by his neighbors, "Gentleman Bob." "Ramrod" Johnson walked too stiffly and carried himself with too much dignity to suit the tastes of his frontier neighbors. A hot-tempered constable became known as "Pot" Williams because he crashed a pot over a man's head in the heat of an argument.

Most cowboys have a nickname. Charles Goodnight, king of the early cattlemen, was called by the Indians the "Leopard-Coat Man" because of a vest of spotted wildcat hide he wore in the wars against them. "Hell and High-Water" was named after his favorite oath.[12] "Eat 'Em Up" Jake was so dubbed after being accused of having a card up his sleeve during a poker game. He ordered a sandwich, slipped the card between the two slices of bread, and ate it.[13] There were "Buckshot" Gallagher, the "Pitchfork Kid" (Bill Parks), a roping champion from the

Pitchfork outfit in King County, "Monkey John," and "Peckerwood" Pete. . . .

The sporting ladies of the frontier resorts used no family names but were well distinguished by fanciful monickers: There were "Pin Head Sue," "Hop Fiend Nel," "Scarface Sal," "Rocking Chair Annie," "Bloomer Jane," "Blonde Rabbit," "Kate with Bobbed Hair," "Miss One Fin," etc., etc.

A noted Indian leader became known as Chief "Iron Shirt" because he possessed a steel breastplate. With this advantageous equipment, he never missed a chance to show his less fortunate followers that he was "bullet proof" by conspicuously exposing himself to the fire of battle; that is, until another warrior, Chief Pock Mark, drew a bead on him above his magic shield—between the eyes, to be exact.

In Western "literature," a preacher was often referred to as a "sky pilot." Individual exhorters have taken on equally as colorful titles. One Negro resident of the State Penitentiary at Huntsville (an evangelist who had to assume a more localized ministry due to confinement growing out of a murder charge) became known far and wide as "Sin-Killer."

PLACE NAMES

Texans likewise have shown characteristic imagination and color in selecting place names, as for instance:

"Elgin," a cleaned-up version of "Hell Again." When the railroad was laid through this locale, a determined faction decided they would not have it. They shot the lights out of the first trains that came through. It became a cus-

★

tom for the trainmen to warn the passengers when approaching this place: "We're going to have Hell again!" In time the shooting stopped but the place continued to be referred to as "Hell Again," usually pronounced "Hell 'gin." When a station was built it was decided that such an appellation would not appeal to real estate buyers, so the name written on the depot was "Elgin."

Many names bespeak of grim beginnings:

Hempstead was so notorious for violent deaths that for many years it was commonly referred to as Six-shooter Junction.

Fiddlers were responsible for names given to at least two towns. James Harvey Litton told the story of origin of "Hog Eye":

"Our home was christened Hog-Eye by the merest accident. A strolling fiddler played for an old-fashioned dance (at Litton's house). He knew only one tune—"Hog Eye" —and played it all evening. The word became a byword in the neighborhood and cannot be discarded."

Blackjack Grove was named for a local fiddler whose favorite tune he called "Blackjack Grove." The name was later shortened to Blackjack, but later on changed to Cumby.

Galveston, according to modern story, derived from "Gal-with-a-vest-on." In this resort of bathing beaches and bare legs, this account is not frowned upon by the Chamber of Commerce. Actually, history books say the town was named for a Viceroy of Mexico, named Galvez; but more people look at the Chamber of Commerce bathing-beauty posters than look at history books. So we may as well forget about the stuffy, high-collared Spanish viceroy.

Sometimes, it appears, the town namers were hard pressed for a title. Several strangely sounding names are words spelled backwards. In Jasper County, a sawmill man named Gilmer, wanted to name the milltown after himself, but upon finding that Texas already had one Gilmer, he reversed the letters of his name and called the town "Remlig."

The Southern Pacific Railroad refers to its road as the "Sunset Route." One of its pumping stations in Brewster County is called "Tesnus," Sunset spelled backwards.

When the founding fathers of Razor had been turned down on a first suggestion for the name of a post office, one citizen adopted the title of the first object he saw—a plug of tobacco bearing the brand name of "Razor." The post office officials accepted the name.

Citizens of Lee County had a practice of leaving their letters at Brown's Mill with a dime in the box for carrying charges. When enough dimes had accumulated to pay a mail carrier, one would take the letters to the nearest post office. Finally, the citizens got a post office of their own. They could think of no name more appropriate than Dime Box.

When the railroad company started surveying a route across John Pierce's ranch, he was asked what he thought of a station in that country. He shouted: "Thank God, that would be a blessing." As a token of thanksgiving for the new convenience, he proposed the name "Thank God" for the station. The railroad officials considered this too irreverent. They compromised on the name "Blessing."

Some names were generally considered of such lowly and embarrassing origin that they were later changed:

★

Hide Town was appropriately designated; but when the tough old buffalo hunters and skinners moved out, and the smell of hides and the sight of bleached bones disappeared, the population decided the community needed a more respectable title. It was renamed "Snyder."

Lick Skillet got its name from a pioneer kitchen process: Children often sopped the skillet with a biscuit, then turned it over to a hound to lick. It is said that, with the advent of broiled steaks, the townspeople became self-conscious and took the name "Pilot Grove."

Hog Town was considered too poor and lowly a name for a prosperous oil town. A native justice of the peace had a daughter with a much more beautiful and elevated name. So the town was named "Desdemona" for her.

Bovina was first known as Bull Town. When the Santa Fé built across the XIT, it put in a switch for unloading cottonseed for cattle feed. The ranchmen had recently imported some gentle Hereford bulls from Missouri. The bulls hung around the switch to pick up the spillings. Then they would lie down on the tracks to chew their cuds. No amount of whistle-blowing and bell-ringing would get them up to let the trains pass. Usually, the trains had to stop while a brakeman prodded the bulls off the tracks. The switch had no official name, but every railroad man on the line referred to the place as Bull Town. This was considered a too vulgar terminology to use in the presence of ladies, so it went on the map as Bovina—the town characterized by lazy bulls.

On occasion the name givers merely added to Indian ingenuity. Wichita Falls means "Waist-deep Falls," so named by an Indian maiden who was given the honor of measuring the depth of the Wichita River for a group of braves returning to camp from a hunt. The hunters found the river on a rise and wanting to know its depth, the Wichita maiden was complimented by being selected to test the depth for them. As she raised her skirt and tripped into the stream she called in her tribal tongue, "Ankle-deep," then "calf-deep," "thigh-deep," and then as she reached the deepest part she called "Wachita." The Indian braves were not unimaginative when it came to complimenting the girls. The word "Falls," for some unknown reason, was added by white buffalo hunters.

A complete list of unique and colorful names would be too long, but to mention a few, there are Poverty Slant, Shake Rag, Gourd Neck, Frog Level, Flat Heel, Short Pone, Nip-and-Tuck, Steal Easy, Possum Trot, and Po Boy.

SIGNS

Texas individualism has been vividly expressed in signs. This one hung on a saloon and dance hall in Fort Griffin called "The Bee Hive":

> Within this hive we're all alive
> Good whisky makes us funny;
> So if you're dry, come in and try
> The flavor of our honey.

Many of the early immigrants lost everything they had in Texas except their sense of humor. One disappointed

★

farmer nailed this notice upon the door of his dugout before leaving the country:

> One hundred miles to water
> Twenty miles to wood
> Six inches to hell.
> God bless our home
> Gone to live with the wife's folks.

Sign on an eastbound wagon, after the drought of 1886 and 1887:

> In God we trusted; went West and got busted.

Another one:

> Last fall came from Rackin Sack
> Got sorry and now go rackin back.

Grimness and humor often went into the same sign. This one was found pinned to the clothing of a body dangling from a cottonwood tree: "In some respects this is a very bad man. In other respects he is a damn sight worse."

No wonder Texas was settled in a hurry. It was not hard to believe an advertisement like this one displayed in an old hotel:

> Come to Van Horn to live
> The climate is so healthy
> We had to shoot a man
> To start a grave yard.

Managers of élite frontier resorts of the rowdy 80's often advised their patrons thus: "Don't shoot the piano player; he's doing the best he can."

Sign on Roy Bean's establishment at Langtry:

THE JERSEY LILY

SALOON   COURT HOUSE

Judge Roy Bean—The Law West of the Pecos

Justice of the Peace   Whisky Wine and Beer

Inside hung this motto: "Argumentum Adjudicum," which Bean translated for wondering visitors: "Don't argue with the judge!"

Badman King Fisher stuck up this pointed warning at a road fork near his home: "This is King Fisher's road. Take the other." And that's exactly what most people did.

During a business depression one merchant, probably with more wit than business, drove a buggy, in a town parade, bearing this sign: "Our store sells no goods on Sunday—and very little the rest of the week."

Even the livery stables stuck up signs:

> Whip light, drive slow
> Pay cash or don't go.

For the benefit of the tobacco-chewing brethren, this one was posted at the entrance on an Austin church by the pastor:

> Ye chewers of that noxious weed
> Which grows on earth's most cursed sod

★

Be pleased to clean your filthy mouths
Outside the sacred House of God
Throw out your "plug and cavendish"
Your "pig tail," "twist" and "honey dew"
And not presume to spit upon
The pulpit, aisles or in the pew.

Donald Day tells of a laundry located next to a church displaying its denominational faith and its pastor's name in huge glaring lights. The laundry, in keeping with the spirit of the locale, put up a sign of its own which read:

CLEANLINESS IS NEXT TO GODLINESS

You keep your soul clean—we'll keep your clothes clean.[14]

EPITAPHS

Texans have been ingenious and humorous even unto death—as is illustrated by epitaphs written of the departed.

This inscription was found over the grave of a cowboy who lost his life fighting Indians along the Goodnight Trail:

He was young, and brave, and fair,
But the Indians raised his hair.

Along the trails there was no time for meditative poets to think up fine phrases, nor were there books from which to copy models. Possibly no acquaintance would ever pass that way again to write inscriptions at a later date.

Another Trailside inscription:

> Here lies the body of Jeems Hambrick
>> who was accidently shot
> on the banks of the pacus river
>> by a young man
> he was accidently shot with one of the large
> colt's revolver with no stopper for the cock
> to rest on it was one of the old-fashion kind
> brass mounted and of such is the kingdom of
> heaven.[15]

On a gravestone in the Oakwood Cemetery in Jefferson is this rhyme:

> Remember, friend, as you pass by,
> As you are now, so once was I,
> As I am now, so you must be,
> Prepare for death and eternity.

The story is told that a wag wrote in charcoal underneath this inscription:

> "Be still, my friend, and rest content,
> Till I find out just where you went."

Other epitaphs in the Jefferson cemetery:

> Budded on earth, Blooming in Heaven.
> God loveth a cheerful giver.
> She hath done what she could.

★

To a sheriff:

> "Shoot-'em-up Jake
> Ran for sheriff, 1872
> Ran for sheriff, 1876
> Buried, 1876.

To a lawyer:

> God works wonders now and then;
> Here lies a lawyer and an honest man.

The frontiersmen made jokes about unpleasant things. Here is an epitaph to a gambler:

> Played five aces,
> Now playing a harp.

Epitaph proposed for tombstone of Gambler Charles Storms, killed by Luke Short:

> He had sand in his craw,
> But was slow on the draw,
> So they laid him out under the daisies.

It is told that a cattle rustler, a running-iron artist, had this epitaph, explaining the cause of his death: "Too Many Irons in the Fire."

Badman Lame Johnny, of the enormous mouth, was hanged by vigilantes—who did not lose their sense of humor in arranging his demise. They placed this epitaph over his grave:

Lame Johnny:
Stranger, pass gently o'er this sod:
If he opens his mouth, you're gone, by God.

Beside a road near Bandera Pass, this inscription, carved in crude letters on a flat stone stood over a rock-covered mound: "Me Injun, Let me be."

Notes

CHAPTER I

1. Frederick L. Olmstead, *A Journey Through Texas* (New York, 1857), p. 382.

2. *Ibid.*, p. 107.

3. *Ibid.*, p. 79.

4. For Parker's report, see *Trip to the West and Texas* (Concord, 1835).

5. Noah Smithwick, *The Evolution of a State* (Austin, 1900), p. 15.

6. J. C. Mann, "When My Grandfather Took the Trail to Texas," in *Parade of the Pioneers*, ed. Otho Anne Hanscom (Dallas, 1935), p. 136.

7. Smithwick, *op. cit.*, p. 18.

8. *Ibid.*, p. 330.

9. *Ibid.*, p. 143.

10. Curtis Bishop and Bascom Giles, *Lots of Land* (Austin, 1949), p. 199.

11. *See* J. Evetts Haley, *Charles Goodnight* (Norman, 1949), p. 292.

12. Philip Ashton Rollins, *The Cowboy* (New York, 1922), p. 331.

13. Jim Feagin, *Fifty Years Under the Bench in Texas* (San Antonio, 1950), p. 103.

14. Olcutt Sanders, "Partners to Your Places" in *The Sky Is My Tipi*, ed. Mody C. Boatright (Dallas, 1949), p. 219.

15. *Ibid.*, pp. 220–21.

16. *Ibid.*, p. 222.

17. A. W. Eddins, "Anecdotes from the Brazos Bottoms," in *Straight Texas*, ed. J. Frank Dobie and Mody C. Boatright (Austin, 1937), pp. 93–94.

18. Smithwick, *op. cit.*, pp. 66–67.

19. T. U. Taylor, "James Harvey Litton, A Pioneer," *Frontier Times*, VII, 522 (September, 1930).

20. Stanley Vestal, *Short Grass Country* (New York, 1941), p. 103.

21. Rollins, *op. cit.*, p. 70.

22. Shine Philips, *Big Spring* (New York, 1945), p. 226.

23. Rollins, *op. cit.*, p. 76.

24. A. B. McDonald, *Hands Up* (New York, 1927), p. 114.

CHAPTER II

1. Smithwick, *The Evolution of A State* (Austin, 1900), p. 16.

2. *Ibid.*, p. 76.

3. N. L. Spence, "A Cathedral of Pines," in *Parade of the Pioneers*, ed. Otho Anne Hanscom (Dallas, 1935), p. 96.

4. Julia Roberts, "Chased by a Panther," *Ibid.*, pp. 51–52.

5. A. A. Parker, *Trip to Texas and the West* (Concord, 1835), p. 152.

6. Oran Warder Nolen, *Galloping Down the Texas Trail* (Odem, 1847), p. 97.

7. Wallace Franks, "Many Rattlesnakes," *Frontier Times*, XX, 43 (November, 1942).

8. Quoted by J. Evetts Haley, in *Charles Goodnight* (Norman, 1949), pp. 427–28.

9. George Stimpson, *A Book About a Thousand Things* (New York, 1946), p. 480.

10. Quoted by Laura V. Hamner in *Amarillo News and Globe* E 30 (August 14, 1938).

★

11. Olmstead, *A Journey Through Texas* (New York, 1857), p. 309.

12. See Stimpson, *op. cit.*, p. 414.

13. August Santleben, *A Texas Pioneer.* Excerpt republished in *Frontier Times*, XVII, 476 (September, 1940).

14. Nolen, *op. cit.*, pp. 99–100.

15. Martha Odell, "The Hope and the Rattlesnakes," *Frontier Times*, XXIV, 422 (May, 1947).

16. Philip Ashton Rollins, *The Cowboy* (New York, 1922), p. 178.

17. James A. McKenna, *Black Range Tales* (New York, 1936), p. 22.

18. *Ibid.*, p. 28.

19. Olive K. Dixon, *Life of "Billy" Dixon* (Dallas, 1927), p. 74.

20. McKenna, *op. cit.*, p. 20.

21. Vestal, *Short Grass Country* (New York, 1941), p. 160.

22. McKenna, *op. cit.*, p. 18.

23. Oren Arnold, *Wild Life in the Southwest* (Dallas, 1935), p. 119.

24. Vestal, *op. cit.*, pp. 154–55.

25. *Ibid.*, 154–55; Haley, *op. cit.*, p. 427.

26. J. Evetts Haley, *Jeff Milton a Good Man with a Gun* (Norman, 1949), p. 42.

27. Quoted by Stuart N. Lake in *Wyatt Earp Frontier Marshal* (New York, 1931), p. 53.

28. For accounts of Belisle, *see* John G. Belisle, *History of Sabine Parish, Louisiana* (Many, 1912), pp. 45–47; N. Bossu, *Travels Through that Part of North America Formerly Called Louisiana,* tr. John Reinhold Foster (London, 1771), I, 332–46; Sam Houston Dixon, *Romance and Tragedy of Texas History* (Houston, 1924), pp. 17–18; Homer S. Thrall, *A Pictorial History of Texas* (St. Louis, 1879), p. 90; H. Yoakum, *History of Texas* (New York, 1855), pp. 69–71.

29. For accounts of the Casner-Sostenes affair, *see* John L. McCarty, *Maverick Town, the Story of Old Tascoso* (Norman, 1946), pp. 19–34; Haley, *Charles Goodnight*, pp. 284–89.

30. McKenna, *op. cit.*, pp. 58–59.

31. Henry Ford, "Some Early Brown County History," *Brownwood Bulletin* (July 29, 1909). Republished in *Frontier Times*, XXVIII, 15 (October, 1950).

32. J. Wright Mooar and James Winford Hunt in *Parade of the Pioneers*, p. 189.

33. Olive K. Dixon, *op. cit.*, pp. 197–98.

CHAPTER III

1. For first hand description, *see* J. Taylor Allen, *Early Pioneer Days in Texas* (Dallas, 1918), pp. 29–31.

2. Henry Ford, "Some Early Brown County History, *Brownwood Bulletin* (July 29, 1909). Republished in *Frontier Times*, XXVIII, 13 (October, 1950).

3. Allen, *op. cit.*, p. 26.

4. McKenna, *Black Range Tales* (New York, 1936), p. 177.

5. Noah Smithwick, *The Evolution of a State* (Austin, 1900), p. 242.

6. Joe Chapman, "An Old Frontiersman Tells His Experience," in *The Trail Drivers of Texas*, com. and ed. J. Marvin Hunter (Nashville, 1925), p. 414.

7. Richard I. Dodge, *Thirty Years Among Our Wild Indians* (Hartford, 1883), p. 543.

8. Allen, *op. cit.*, p. 12.

9. Dodge, *op. cit.*, p. 595.

10. Ernest Wallace and E. Adamson Hoebel, *The Comanches* (Norman, 1952), p. 61.

11. Andy Adams, *The Log of a Cowboy* (Boston and New York, 1927), p. 26.

12. J. Frank Dobie, *The Mustangs* (Boston, 1952), p. 292.

13. *Ibid.*, p. 307.

14. *Ibid.*, p. 201.

15. J. Frank Dobie, "The Wild and Free Mustangs," *Country Gentleman* (October, 1952).

16. Dobie, *The Mustangs*, p. 112.

17. *Ibid.*, p. 230.

★

18. Dobie, "The Wild and Free Mustangs," *Country Gentleman* (October, 1952).

19. Dobie, *The Mustangs*, p. 188.

20. "A Little Bay Mare Called Ginger," *Frontier Times*, XXI, 313–320 (May, 1944).

21. J. C. Hart, "Callahan County Pioneer Passes Away," *Frontier Times*, XXIV, 467 (July, 1947).

22. *The Cowboy* (New York, 1922), p. 287.

23. Harry Hubert, " 'Old Trickham' of Cattle Trail Days," *Frontier Times*, XXVII, 149 (February, 1950).

24. Rollins, *op. cit.*, p. 281.

25. Dobie, *The Mustangs*, p. 302.

26. Adopted from "Ad. Lawrence's Ride," *Texas Scrap Book*, com. D. W. C. Baker (New York, 1875), pp. 342–344.

27. Dobie, *A Vaquero of the Brush Country* (New York, 1929), p. 9.

28. For account of Sandoval, *see* N. A. Jennings, *A Texas Ranger* (Dallas, 1930), pp. 74–90.

29. Rollins, *op. cit.*, p. 61.

30. William MacLeod Raine, *Guns of the Frontier* (Cleveland, 1946), p. 145.

31. *Mavericks* (Pasadena, 1942), p. 175.

32. J. C. Duval, *Early Times in Texas* (Austin, 1892), p. 114.

33. *Ibid.*, p. 117.

34. Frost Woodhull, "Folk-Lore Shooting," *Frontier Times*, XXIX, 254 (June, 1952). Republished from Publications of the Texas Folklore Society, Vol. IX.

35. *Op. cit.*, p. 14.

36. J. Evetts Haley, *Charles Goodnight* (Norman, 1949), p. 113.

37. A. B. MacDonald, *Hands Up!* (New York, 1927), p. 282.

38. George D. Hendricks, *The Bad Man of the West* (San Antonio, 1950), p. 56.

39. Jan Fortune and Jean Burton, *Elizabeth Ney* (New York, 1943), p. 258.

40. John William Rogers, *The Lusty Texans of Dallas* (New York, 1951), p. 87.

41. *Ibid.*, p. 25; Lucy C. Trent, *John Neely Bryan* (Dallas, 1936), p. 1.

42. James B. Gillett, *Six Years with the Texas Rangers* (New Haven, 1925), p. 35.

43. George W. Kendall, "Geo. W. Kendall in Tragic Enterprise," *Frontier Times*, XXIV, 522 (September, 1947).

44. *Op. cit.*, p. 287.

45. *See* Dobie, *A Vaquero of the Brush Country*, p. 228.

46. *Ibid.*, p. 231.

47. *Galloping Down the Texas Trail* (Odem, 1947), p. 72.

48. Oren Arnold, quoting Oliver Jones in *Wild Life of the Southwest* (Dallas, 1935), p. 4.

49. *Ibid.*, p. 7.

50. Dobie, *The Mustangs*, p. 125.

51. *Op. cit.*, pp. 168–69.

CHAPTER IV

1. Lone Cowboy (New York, 1930), p. 262.

2. Oran Warder Nolen, *Galloping Down the Texas Trail* (Odem, Texas, 1947), p. 69.

3. *Ibid.*

4. J. Frank Dobie, *A Vaquero of the Brush Country* (New York, 1929), p. 19.

5. *See* W. E. Cureton, "Drove a Herd Over the Trail to California," in *The Trail Drivers of Texas*, com. and ed. J. Marvin Hunter (Nashville, 1925), p. 55.

6. "No Room in the Tent for Polecats," in *The Trail Drivers of Texas*, p. 659.

7. *See* George W. Saunders, "Reflections of the Trail," in *The Trail Drivers of Texas*, p. 435.

8. *See* R. T. Millard, "The Latch String Is on the Outside," in *The Trail Drivers of Texas*, p. 599; G. W. Mills, *op. cit.*, p. 233.

★

9. *Mavericks* (Pasadena, 1947), p. 22.

10. "Twice Across the Plains in Fourteen Months," in *The Trail Drivers of Texas*, p. 326.

11. P. 96.

12. J. Evetts Haley, *Charles Goodnight* (Norman, 1949), p. 250.

13. *Amarillo News Globe*, E., p. 30 (August 14, 1938).

14. Dobie, *op. cit.*, p. 99.

15. *The Trail Drivers of Texas*, p. 1038.

16. *See* J. M. Hankins, "Reminiscences of Old Trail Driving," in *The Trail Drivers of Texas*, p. 114.

17. *From the Plains to the Pulpit* (Goose Creek, 1907), p. 34.

18. "The Experience of an Old Trail Driver," in *The Trail Drivers of Texas*, p. 306.

19. L. B. Anderson, "A Few Thrilling Incidents in My Experiences on the Trail," in *The Trail Drivers of Texas*, p. 207.

20. Quoted by Haley, *op. cit.*, p. 253.

21. See S. D. Houston, "When a Girl Masqueraded as a Cowboy and Spent Four Months on the Trail," in *The Trail Drivers of Texas*, p. 73.

22. *Op. cit.*, p. 205.

23. W. F. Thompson, "My Trip up the Trail," in *The Trail Drivers of Texas*, p. 537.

24. "The Latch String Is on the Outside," in *The Trail Drivers of Texas*, p. 598.

25. *Op. cit.*, p. 204.

26. Dobie, *op. cit.*, p. 34.

27. Haley, *op. cit.*, pp. 255–56.

28. W. T. Jackman, "Where They Put a Trail Boss in Jail," in *The Trail Drivers of Texas*, p. 860.

29. "Some Texas Brands Were Puns," *Frontier Times*, XVIII, 490 (August, 1941).

30. *Ibid.*

31. Frank Reeves, Sr., "Story of Cattle Brands," in *A Century of Texas Cattle Brands* (Amarillo, 1936), p. 17.

32. Oren Arnold, *Sun in Your Eyes* (Albuquerque, 1947), p. 65.

33. An oft-repeated story of varying versions. For a comparatively recent account, *see* Robert J. Casey, *The Texas Border* (New York, 1950), pp. 299–300.

CHAPTER V

1. Quoted by William Ranson Hogan, *The Republic of Texas* (Norman, 1946), p. 227.

2. Frederick L. Olmstead, *A Journey Through Texas* (New York, 1857), p. 301.

3. Noah Smithwick, *The Evolution of a State* (Austin, 1900), p. 18.

4. *Op. cit.*, p. 300.

5. Big Foot Wallace's recipe.

6. John William Rogers, *The Lusty Texans of Dallas* (New York, 1951), p. 177.

7. "Traded Farm for a Sack of Coffee," *Dallas News* (December 20, 1931). Republished in *Frontier Times*, IX, 251–254 (March, 1932).

8. *Mavericks* (Pasadena, 1947), pp. 145, 149.

9. *See* C. L. Sonnichsen, *Cowboys and Cattle Kings* (Norman, 1950), p. 101.

10. C. L. Ford, "Trading Foodstuffs in the Early Days," *Parade of the Pioneers*, p. 34.

CHAPTER VI

1. John C. Duval, *The Adventures of Big Foot Wallace* (Macon, 1871), pp. 219–220.

2. Noah Smithwick, *The Evolution of a State* (Austin, 1900), p. 147.

3. Mody C. Boatright, *Folk Laughter on the American Frontier* (New York, 1949), pp. 59–60.

4. W. B. Foster, in *The Trail Drivers of Texas*, com. and ed. J. Marvin Hunter (Nashville, 1925), p. 659.

5. J. Frank Dobie, *A Vaquero of the Brush Country* (New York, 1929), pp. 236–239.

6. *Jeff Milton: A Good Man with a Gun* (Norman, 1949), p. 46.

★

7. *Ibid.*, p. 39.

8. "Some News Items of Long Ago," *Frontier Times*, XVIII, 306 (April, 1941).

9. Shine Philips, *Big Spring* (New York, 1945), p. 206.

10. A. W. Eddins, "Ancedotes from the Brazos Bottoms," in *Straight Texas*, ed. J. Frank Dobie and Mody C. Boatright (Austin, 1937), p. 89.

11. Adopted from "Sham Hays and His Bull Race," in *Frontier Times*, XVII, 128–29 (December, 1939). Quoted from *The Western Stock Journal* (December 2, 1873).

CHAPTER VII

1. There are innumerable verses of as many versions on this subject. See *Cowboy Songs and Other Frontier Ballads*, collected by John A. Lomax and Alan Lomax (New York, 1938), pp. 135–136; *A Treasury of American Folklore*, ed. B. A. Botkin (New York, 1944), pp. 61–66; Mody C. Boatright, *Folk Laughter on the American Frontier* (New York, 1949), pp. 29–30; J. Frank Dobie, "Ballads and Songs of the Frontier Folk," Texas Folklore Society Publication, VI, 149.

2. Alfred Henry Lewis, *Wolfville Days* (New York, 1902), pp. 273–274. Quoted by Mody C. Boatright, *op. cit.*, pp. 24–25.

3. Philip Ashton Rollins, *The Cowboy* (New York, 1922), p. 53.

4. Emerson Bennett, *Mike Fink: A Legend of the Ohio* (Cincinnati, 1848), pp. 24–25, 83. Quoted by B. A. Botkins, *op. cit.*, p. 57.

5. Mody C. Boatright, *op. cit.*, p. 29.

6. *Ibid.*, p. 88.

7. *Amarillo Sunday News and Globe*, F, p. 28 (August 14, 1938).

8. Richard Dorson, *Davy Crockett, American Comic Legend* (New York, 1939), pp. 29–30.

9. Stuart N. Lake, *Wyatt Earp, Frontier Marshal* (New York, 1931), p. 69.

10. *Hands Up* (New York, 1927), p. 137.

11. Lomax, *op. cit.*, p. 61.

12. Boyce House, *Roundup of Texas Humor* (San Antonio, 1949), p. 215.

13. Mody C. Boatright, "Backwoods Belles," in *From Backwoods to Border*, ed. Mody C. Boatright and Donald Day (Austin and Dallas, 1943), pp. 66, 67, 78.

14. *Ibid.*, p. 69.

15. Adopted from Boatright, *Folk Laughter on the American Frontier* (New York, 1944), p. 34.

16. George D. Hendricks, *The Bad Man of the West* (San Antonio, 1942), p. 68.

17. *Ibid.*

18. A. B. Macdonald, *op. cit.*, p. 220.

19. Frost Woodhull, "Folk-Lore Shooting," *Frontier Times*, XXIX, 252 (June, 1952). Quoted from Texas Folklore Society Publication, Vol.

20. *Ibid.*, p. 254.

21. McDonald, *op. cit.*, p. 92.

22. J. Frank Dobie, "Stories in Texas Place Names," in *Straight Texas*, ed. J. Frank Dobie and Mody C. Boatright (Austin, 1937), p. 60.

23. Woodhull, *op. cit.*, p. 254.

24. McDonald, *op. cit.*, p. 113.

25. Woodhull, *op. cit.*, p. 252. For account of affair, *see* Ross Phares, "Triggerhappy Ben Thompson," in *Preview of Texas* (April, 1951), p. 17.

26. McDonald, *op. cit.*, p. 73.

27. *Ibid.*, p. 42.

28. *Ibid.*, p. 70; Woodhull, *op. cit.*, p. 252.

29. Hendricks, *op. cit.*, p. 66.

CHAPTER VIII

1. For further uses of rawhide, *see* J. Frank Dobie, "Rawhide Has Faithfully Served Texas," *Frontier Times*, XIX, 133 (January, 1942); and Edgar Beecher Bronson, *The Red-Blooded Heroes of the Frontier* (New York, 1910), p. 7.

★

2. Macum Phelan, *A History of Early Methodism in Texas, 1817–1866* (Nashville, 1924), pp. 20–21.

3. W. T. Jackman, "Where They Put a Trail Boss in Jail," in *The Trail Drivers of Texas*, com. and ed. J. Marvin Hunter (Nashville, 1925), p. 861.

4. *A History of Jefferson, Marion County, Texas* (Jefferson, n.d.), p. 15.

5. Jack Harper and John Newbern, *Odd Texas* (Dallas, 1936), p. 74.

6. *Ibid.*, p. 76.

7. Account taken from Noah Smithwick, *The Evolution of a State* (Austin, 1900), pp. 210–213.

8. S. O. Young, *True Stories of Old Houston and Houstonians* (Galveston, 1913), p. 210.

9. Jack Harper and John Newbern, *op. cit.*, p. 69.

10. *Ibid.*, p. 120.

11. J. C. Duval, *Early Times in Texas* (Austin, 1902), pp. 114–115.

12. John C. Duval, *The Adventures of Big Foot Wallace* (Macon, 1871), pp. 152–153.

13. J. W. Wilbarger, *Indian Depredations in Texas* (Austin, 1889), pp. 107–109.

14. *Ibid.*, pp. 272–274.

15. W. F. Cody, *Story of the Great West and Camp Fire Chats* (Chicago, 1902), pp. 276–280.

16. Wilbarger, *op. cit.*, p. 147.

17. *Ibid.*, pp. 456–457.

18. For an excellent treatment of Praxiteles' Swan Legend, *see* John W. Thomason, Jr., *Lone Star Preacher* (New York, 1941).

CHAPTER IX

1. Noah Smithwick, *The Evolution of a State* (Austin, 1900), p. 127.

2. *Ibid.*, p. 282.

3. *Lots of Land* (Austin, 1949), p. 238.

224

4. *Wyatt Earp, Frontier Marshal* (Cambridge, 1931), pp. 59–60.

5. *Ibid.*, pp. 60–61.

6. J. M. Carroll, *A History of Texas Baptists* (Dallas, 1923), p. 125.

7. Mody C. Boatright, *Folk Laughter on the American Frontier* (New York, 1949), pp. 143–44.

8. "Observations and Experiences of Bygone Days," in *The Trail Drivers of Texas*, com. and ed. J. Marvin Hunter (Nashville, 1925), p. 161.

9. *A Texas Ranger* (Dallas, 1930), p. 25.

10. James Farber, *Texas, C. S. A.* (New York, 1947), pp. 53–54.

CHAPTER X

1. *Wyatt Earp* (New York, 1931), pp. 75–76.

2. Wyatt Earp said that Masterson was the best poker player he ever saw in action. *Ibid.*, p. 63.

3. Quoted by Jess Guy Smith in *Heroes of the Saddlebags* (Austin, 1951), p. 12.

4. *The Texas Republic*, p. 26.

5. S. O. Young, *True Stories of Old Houston and Houstonians* (Galveston, 1913), pp. 154–155.

6. August 14, 1938.

7. Stuart N. Lake, *Wyatt Earp*, p. 109.

8. Curtis Bishop and Bascomb Giles, *Lots of Land* (Austin, 1949), p. 135.

9. John William Roger, *Lusty Texans of Dallas*, p. 144.

10. *Op. cit.*, p. 157.

11. J. Evetts Haley, *Jeff Milton, A Good Man with a Gun*, p. 47.

12. *A Texas Ranger*, p. 148.

13. Donald Day, *Big Country: Texas* (New York, 1947), p. 58.

14. Young, *op. cit.*, p. 162–163.

15. *Ibid.*

16. Noah Smithwick, *The Evolution of a State* (Austin, 1900), p. 75.

★

17. Richard I. Dodge, *Our Wild Indians* (Hartford, 1883), pp. 341–342.

CHAPTER XI

1. George Plunkett Red (Mrs. S. C. Red), *The Medicine Man in Texas* (Houston, 1930), p. 13.

2. *Ibid.*, pp. 23–24 (Second and third sentences of quotation are rearranged for clarity).

3. Baxar Archives I, 52. From a mimeographed summary distributed by the University of Texas Free News Service, n.d.

4. Carlos E. Castaneda, *Our Catholic Heritage in Texas* (Austin, 1942), V, 204.

5. Baxar Archives, *loc. cit.*

6. Red, *op. cit.*, p. 15.

7. William Ransom Hogan, *The Texas Republic* (Norman, 1946), p. 244.

8. Baxar Archives, *loc. cit.*

9. *The (Houston) Morning Star*, August 29, 1843. Quoted in Red, *op. cit.*, pp. 90–91.

10. Baxar Archives, *loc. cit.*

11. *Ibid.*

12. S. O. Young, *True Stories of Old Houston and Houstonians* (Galveston, 1913), p. 150.

13. *A Journey Through Texas* (New York, 1857), p. 374.

14. Oran Warder Nolen, "Some Odd Mexican Customs, in *From Hell to Breakfast*, ed. Mody C. Boatright and Donald Day (Austin and Dallas, 1944), p. 58.

15. "Times Have Changed," *Frontier Times*, XXVIII, 311 (August, 1951).

16. Frost Woodhull, "Ranch Remedies," in *Man, Bird, and Beast*, ed. J. Frank Dobie (Austin, 1930), p. 16.

17. Quoted in Red, *op. cit.*, p. 90.

18. Charles Goodnight said that was a "sure cure."

19. Red, *op. cit.*, p. 313.

20. *Ibid.*, pp. 201–203.

21. Quoted by Red, *op. cit.*, p. 88.

22. *Amarillo News and Globe*, F 28 (August 14, 1938).

23. Noah Smithwick, *The Evolution of a State* (Austin, 1900), p. 69.

24. *Ibid.*, p. 296.

25. *Ibid.*, p. 312.

26. Red, *op. cit.*, p. 80. *See further* p. 91.

27. *Ibid.*, p. 94.

28. *Ibid.*, p. 88.

CHAPTER XII

1. Stephen F. Austin Papers Series II, 23. From a mimeographed summary distributed by University of Texas Free News Service, n.d.

2. Noah Smithwick, *The Evolution of a State* (Austin, 1900), p. 98.

3. *Ibid.*, pp. 146–147.

4. Frederick L. Olmstead, *A Journey Through Texas* (New York, 1857), p. 302.

5. Smithwick, *op. cit.*, p. 146.

6. *Op. cit.*, p. 102.

7. *Op. cit.*, pp. 307–308.

8. For example see Stanley Vestal, *Kit Carson* (New York, 1928), p. 110.

9. H. M. Henderson, address delivered before the Texas Landmarks and Historical Association, at the Bluebonnet Hotel, February 13, 1947. Published by *Frontier Times*, XXIV, 403 (May, 1947).

10. S. O. Young, *A Thumb-Nail History of the City of Houston, Texas* (Houston, 1912), p. 122.

11. Smithwick, *op. cit.*, p. 140.

12. *Ibid.*, p. 194.

13. *Op. cit.*, p. 116.

14. *Texas C. S. A.* (New York, 1947), pp. 103–104.

15. This fighting stock is still in Texas. John Randolph, in *Texas Braggs* (Houston, 1950), p. 29, points out that during World War II 14 natives and three adopted sons were awarded Congressional

Medals of Honor, leading all states. Nineteen of the 79 men in the Doolittle raid were Texans. The most decorated soldier of the war was a Texan, Audie Murphy, from Farmerville. Percentagewise, Texas led all states in number of personnel in the Navy, Marines, Air Corps, and Coast Guard. One hundred and forty-four generals and admirals were Texans.

16. Castaneda, *Our Catholic Heritage in Texas* (Austin, 1942), V, 202.

17. *Op. cit.*, p. 104.

18. *Ibid.*, p. 106.

19. *Ibid.*, p. 132.

20. John J. Linn, Reminiscences of Fifty Years in Texas (New York, 1883), p. 264.

21. Olmstead, *op. cit.*, p. 302.

22. Curtis Bishop, *This Day in Texas* (San Angelo, 1948), February 28.

23. A. T. Jackson, "Confederate Gunpowder," *Frontier Times*, XXVIII, 34 (November, 1950).

24. *Op. cit.*, p. 21.

25. *Ibid.*, p. 21.

26. John Warren Hunter, "General Mackenzie Slaughters 1300 Horses," *Frontier Times*, XXX, 232 (April, May, June, 1953).

27. James Farber, *Texas C. S. A.*, p. 71.

28. *Ibid.*, p. 67.

CHAPTER XIII

1. Baxar Archives, I, 27. From a mimeographed summary distributed by the University of Texas Free News Service, n.d.

2. *Ibid.*

3. *Ibid.*

4. *Ibid.*

5. *Ibid.*, p. 50.

6. *Ibid.*, p. 47; *See also* William Ranson Hogan, *The Texas Republic* (Norman, 1946), p. 262.

7. Castaneda, *Our Catholic Heritage in Texas* (Austin, 1942), V, p. 412.

8. *Ibid.*, p. 415.

9. *Ibid.*, pp. 412–13.

10. *Ibid.*, p. 413.

11. *Ibid.*, p. 415.

12. Noah Smithwick, *The Evolution of a State* (Austin, 1900), p. 58.

13. *Amarillo News and Globe* (August 14, 1938).

14. *Ibid.*, A 12.

15. *Ibid.*, A 23.

16. A. W. Eddins, "Anecdotes from the Brazos Bottoms," in *Straight Texas*, ed. J. Frank Dobie and Mody C. Boatright (Austin, 1937), pp. 95–96.

17. Jim Feagin, *Fifty Years Under the Bench in Texas* (San Antonio, 1950), p. 32.

18. C. L. Sonnichsen, *Roy Bean* (New York, 1943), p. 56.

CHAPTER XIV

1. Olive K. Dixon, *The Life of "Billy" Dixon* (Dallas, 1927), p. 100.

2. James Pike, *Scout and Ranger* (Princeton, 1932), p. 65.

3. Jan Fortune and Jean Burton, *Elizabeth Ney* (New York, 1943), p. 270.

4. Shine Philips, *Big Spring* (New York, 1945), p. 79.

5. Joe M. Evans, *A Corral Full of Stories* (El Paso, 1939), p. 50.

6. Supposedly written by General O. O. Howard. See "Jack Davenport, Pioneer Uvalde County Citizen, *Frontier Times*, XXIX, 22 (October, 1951).

7. *A Treasury of Western Folklore*, ed. B. A. Botkin (New York, 1951), p. 234.

8. The original publisher of this sermon is not known. The *Frontier Times*, XVI, 349–351 (May, 1939), among other publications has printed it.

9. In some instances, the origin of nicknames are controversial. A story has reached print to the effect that Big Foot Wallace got his famous nickname because of an "unyielding, life-time search"

★

for a Lipan Indian whose track measured 16 inches in length, in order to get his moccasins. Duval, who wrote a biography of Wallace based mainly upon interviews with his subject and manuscripts written by him, gave this account of the "Big Foot" origin in Wallace's own words: " 'It was while we were prisoners at Mexico City (result of the Mier Expedition) that I acquired the name of "Big Foot," which has stuck to me like Texas mud ever since. . . . Everyone was fitted with a suitable pair [of shoes] except myself; but I searched in vain every shop and *tienda* in the city for even a pair of No. 11's, though 12's fit me best, and finally I had no alternative left me but to buy the leather and have a pair put up on purpose for me by a *Zapatero*, or go barefooted. The Mexicans are generally a small people compared with the Americans, and their feet are still smaller in proportion; consequently, they were much astonished at the size of mine, and from that time forward, as long as I remained in the city, I was known among them as 'Big-Foot.' " *See The Adventures of Big-Foot Wallace* (Macon, 1871), pp. 221–222.

10. J. Marvin Hunter, *A Brief History of Bandera County* (Baird, 1949), p. 18.

11. Stanley Vestal, *Queen of Cowtowns Dodge City* (New York, 1951), p. 273.

12. *Ibid.*, p. 80.

13. *Ibid.*, p. 60.

14. *Big Country, Texas* (New York, 1947), p. 297.

15. *San Diego Herald*, 1854. Quoted by J. Evetts Haley in *Charles Goodnight* (Norman, 1949), p. 186.

★

Index

★

★

★

★

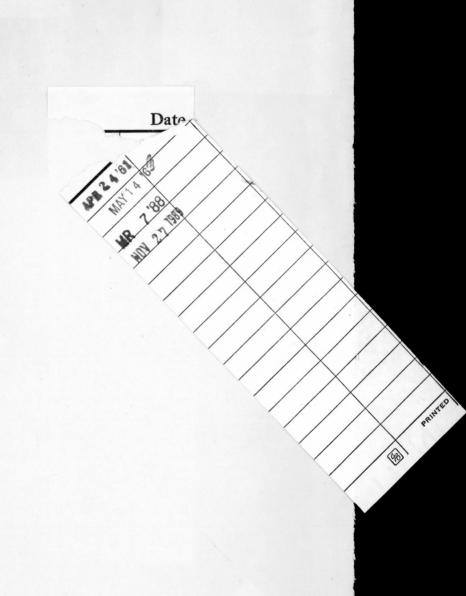